Real
Newport

I sing a city –
glorious Newport!

Twinned with Kutaisi,
rhymed with Rupert...

Newport (Casnewydd-ar-Wysg), Wales' third largest town, a downbeat, working-class place that grew up around the docks at the mouth of the Usk.

Wales: The Rough Guide. Mike Parker and Paul Whitfield.

ann
drysdale

Real
Newport

series editor: peter finch

seren

Seren is the book imprint of
Poetry Wales Press Ltd
57 Nolton Street, Bridgend, Wales
www.seren-books.com

ISBN 978-185411-432-7

A CIP record for this title is available from
the British Library

The publisher works with the financial assistance
of the Welsh Books Council

Printed in Plantin by CPD (Wales, Ebbw Vale)
Cover Photograh: Rex Moreton / Photolibrary Wales

Also in the *Real Wales* series:
Real Cardiff – Peter Finch
Real Cardiff Two – Peter Finch

Coming in 2007:
Real Aberystwyth – Niall Griffiths
Real Swansea – Nigel Jenkins
Real Wrexham – Grahame Davies

CONTENTS

THE POEMS

PREFACE

Newport on the Usk, industrial working town, steel works, docks, dark, in the nineteenth century full of wily entrepreneurs and hoary sons of toil, ruffians in rags, women in shawls, businessmen in stove-pipe hats. It's not that today. Nothing like.

Newport, Wales' first city (as it said for a while on a notice where London coaches arrived at the bus station), steel works and docks closed or diminished, with air you can breathe, and soon to be filled with new roadways and bright bridges and sky – reaching apartment blocks and aluminium and glass. Newport Unlimited, the city's urban regeneration company, has begun its twenty year project to elevate and reinvent the gateway to Wales. The mid-twentieth century wonders of John Frost Square, the mesh of snaking mosaic subways below the repointed but still securely fenced-off castle, the *Lord of the Rings* lookalike Chartist statues opposite the Westgate Hotel, or even that Edwardian masterpiece, the Transporter Bridge, will have nothing on the glories to come.

I'm here in late 2006 checking the town out prior to the completion of Ann Drysdale's *Real Newport,* the book you hold, and already the city's roads are riddled with diversion signs, traffic cones, new kerbing and new paths. Car parks are filled with digging machinery, waste ground is being levelled, battered, and disused red-bricks like the College of Art at Clarence Place are being readied for their transformation into city centre gated apartments, keep your car underground, don't have a garden, be right there where the action is.

The vision is immense. Already the new Usk footbridge, looking like a sculpture of an enormous bike lock, is in place. Stroll from Peter Fink's once massively controversial red *Steel Wave,* past the Riverfront's slew of interconnected silver centre blocks then cross the Usk's mighty and unrepentant muddiness to end up, where, in the boondocks back of Rodney Parade. But that's all up for transformation. Work starts soon.

Newport is divided into fourteen separate yet interconnected developments – Left Bank, East Bank, Hospital District, River East Gateway – making the city sound like something from fantasy fiction. Over the new footbridge (850 tonnes, it took 48 articulated lorries just to deliver the crane which erected it) on the eastern bank's hoardings the whole development is explained to the local population via a series of posters, just like they do in China. In John Frost Square I asked at the Information Bureau if they have a leaflet: they don't. Try the Library. They don't have one either. But online there is an upbeat website with a master plan brochure available for download. Took fifteen seconds. Arrived straight in my living room. Newport in the future already.

The thing about Newport is that despite having historically significant outriders like Caerleon, once the Roman gateway to Wales and now a north eastern suburb, and the remains of a giant hill fort guarding the western approaches (Gaer Hill Fort, overlooking the Ebbw River), the place is actually pretty compact. Population around a third of that of its great rival Cardiff. Knowable, lovable, generous. It's so easy to get from one place to the next. In 1959 in the film *Tiger Bay*, troubled drifter Bronik stepped onto the Transporter Bridge on the Usk's southern reaches and alighted in Loudon Square, Cardiff Docks. That's a trick many have tried since and until the semi–conductor factory produces the working matter transmitter some wag in the University told me they were developing it'll stay that way too.

The city is pretty multi-cultural too. On my walk over the new footbridge and then back across the Newport Bridge to then try, and fail, to get within touching distance of the castle (built fourteenth century, misused as a brewery in the nineteenth, haunt for ne'er-do-wells more recently), I heard at least a dozen languages being spoken. The predominant local accent, as exemplified by Newport's most successful recent export, Goldie Lookin Chain, only rivals that of Cardiff in its ability to cut through trees at twenty paces. Where does it come from? A mixture of Welsh and West Country with a levelling of Irish, or maybe that should be the other way around. An accent of immigrants. Has to be. Look at the population figures: 6657 in 1801, 137,000 today.

Real Newport is an offbeat ramble around some of the things Newport is famous for and around a lot that it is not. It's more a psychogeography than it is a guide book but how you find it will depend a lot on what you already know. It's one of most entertaining handbooks to a Welsh place that's been written. If you are a visitor then this is the volume you want with you on your travels. If you are, rather, a true Newportian, still living here or left and now nostalgic for the place's sounds and smells then *Real Newport* will explain what you didn't know and then bring into full focus that which you did.

In a bookshop somewhere below the Kings Hotel (once the preferred haunt of Van Morrison and dozens of other twentieth-century musical icons, a crown transferred to TJs for the twenty-first century, proving that when it comes to the music biz Newport can certainly show Cardiff a thing or two. Swansea isn't even in the frame), down here among the acres of romance fiction, cookbooks, historical novels, photography handbooks and maps of everywhere in the world bar south Wales, I could find nothing on Wales' newest city. The bloke behind the counter said there wasn't that much demand. Has to be wrong.

I wrote *Real Cardiff* in 2002 and on the back that book's excellent reception wrote *Real Cardiff Two* in 2004. Both titles are published by Seren. In order to roll out the idea across the rest of the conurbations of Wales I have taken on the role of series editor and have contracted with a range of authors, most of whom have some literary experience either as novelists or poets, and put in train what looks already like the unstoppable. Certainly the unfinishable. The pace of change in Wales is currently so great that after the passage of as little as five years locations transform themselves, opinions shift, and perceptions alter totally. Ann Drysdale's *Real Newport* carries on brilliantly the offbeat, anecdotal, historical and completely engaging trail beaten by those first books. Watch your bookshop shelves for more.

Peter Finch
Cardiff, October 2006

INTRODUCTION

NEWPORT THROUGH THE AGES

Oh, Lord – that sounds like one of those grainy old films they used to put on between features in the days when going to the cinema cost one-and-ninepence and the programme planners felt you ought to have a little bit of everything on your plate, like a balanced meal. This would have been the equivalent of the Brussels sprouts. *Settle down and pay attention; it's good for you. If you don't, there'll be no 'Brief Encounter'.*

Newport is a medium-sized city at the mouth of the River Usk. The river is tidal, with a maximum rise second only to the Bay of Fundy in Newfoundland. When the tide is in, a glistening brown ribbon divides the place neatly in two. When it is out, there is an impressive acreage of honest mud. Both are beautiful.

The first record of any settlement on the banks of the Usk was at Caerleon, where the local tribesmen, the Silures, had established a hill fort. This is what the Romans found when they arrived at the end of the first century. And there they stayed until the end of the third. But –

> Before the Roman came to Usk or had to Severn been
> The native folk of Newport, they were nowhere to be seen.
> They did not trade in tablecloths, they did not trade in tin
> They did not live in luxury, they did not live in sin.
> Before the Roman filled his lungs with estuary air
> The native folk of Newport were apparently elsewhere.

When the chroniclers of the eighth century, albeit in pursuit of the truth about King Arthur, referred to Caerleon, it was apparently the only trading port on the Usk. If there was another settlement a couple of miles nearer the mouth of the river, nobody saw fit to mention it, so even if it was there, it can't have amounted to much. Perhaps there were a few huts and even the odd mud-gaitered peasant who muttered and chucked sods at the Roman vessels as they passed by. Perhaps not.

If we may be permitted to venture into legend, we may choose to believe that the first church was built by St Woolos in the seventh century. Even so, that was up on Stow Hill, quite a way above the site of the city and although it has been assimilated now, it would have been quite separate then. Who would venture down onto the noisome flood plain if they didn't have to? Why, even the white bullock that is supposed to have led the saint to his salvation had the mother wit to head uphill.

There seems to have been some sort of settlement in the tenth century. A busy little village, perhaps. Probably a mongrel sort of place, mixing the native Welsh with Anglo Saxons from nearby Mercia. It was this that the Normans found when they turned up at the beginning of the next century and gave it its first recorded name: Novus Burgus. The New Town. They built the first castle, which the locals called Castell Newydd. The New Castle. It was not until the town's charter of 1427 that the name Newporte in Wallia first appeared.

And that was that, really. For the next few centuries nothing much happened. We know from the discovery of the Newport Ship that there was a modicum of maritime trade. Now and again the odd political upheaval or local fracas resulted in a few dwellings burned, the odd bridge knackered and rebuilt, but not much to write home about. People just kept their heads down and got on with the business of living. As in the way of all small towns, corruption occasionally caused scandals and the fortunes of self-appointed gentry rose and fell. People planned vaguely in the way people do in uninteresting times "Ah, brother – come the revolution..." Then, one day, the revolution came.

The nineteenth century Industrial Revolution. It swept Newport up on a great wave of prosperity and manufacturing and left it, at its height, one of the most important places in Britain.

Vast deposits of coal and iron ore were discovered in the Monmouthshire Valleys. Money was made; money that funded the retrieval of the natural treasures and the infrastructure to transport them to the nearest deep-water port for manufacture into commercial products and efficient distribution to the world. Newport's day had come. The population increased tenfold and by the 1830s Newport had become the largest town in Wales. It was known worldwide for its accessible, modern docks and as trade increased, those docks were expanded. In 1914 Newport shipped over six million tons of coal.

And now those docks are almost gone. The steelworks are winding down into streamlined, specialised units employing a fraction of their earlier workforce and the major industries are relocated elsewhere. New enterprises have been coaxed in and have backed out again. A sick, sad entry in the opportunistic publication *Crap Towns* and the grim reference (quoted on the title page) in the *Rough Guide to Wales* mark Newport's sad nadir.

But the river carries a parable: highs and lows are dramatic, but ephemeral. And from the low points, the only way is up again. In

2002, to mark her Golden Jubilee, Her Majesty graciously (and eventually) accorded Newport the status of City, for which it had tried and failed in 1994 and 2000.

A consortium calling itself Newport Unlimited is trying to regenerate the place and little by little good things are happening, despite fearful grumbling at grass-roots level. Pride is stirring. Groups like the Friends of the Newport Ship and tireless local historians are trying to reconstruct all that missing history. What is needed now is something to ignite the touchpaper that will set off the new city like a firework into the future.

Nice thought. To do that will require what the bright new management at the scaled-down steelworks calls a 'culture change'. As they have proved, it can be done, but it will take time.

When I attempted to establish the present population of Newport, I naturally consulted the website of the Office for National Statistics, since this organisation has recently relocated here. The figure currently stands at 135,000. Then I looked at their recruitment site to see how they were selling the city to prospective employees. It begins by telling them it is "only twenty minutes from the Welsh capital, Cardiff, and forty minutes from Bristol. Both are vibrant, cosmopolitan cities with their own unique atmosphere – between them they cater for every conceivable interest, pastime and sport." They go on to extol the Brecon Beacons and the Gower.

Only at the end do they mention the city itself. They seem to have had some difficulty finding anything to say about it. I quote verbatim: "The city centre is approximately two miles from the Office and has a busy rail network and is easily accessible by the regular busy rail network and is easily accessible by the regular bus service" (sic). They didn't even bother to proofread it.

As I say, it will take time.

Newport Song...

Give me a song to sing about the place
And I will do my best to orchestrate it.
Draw me a picture of its homely face
And I will find a way to decorate it.
No one likes Newport, probably because
It's always been defined by what it's not,
Compared with something that it never was
And classified by what it hasn't got.
I shall adopt the city's attitude –
Two fingers to the guidebook on the shelf –
And call upon Saint Woolos and Saint Jude
To show me how to make it sing itself.
Come in with me and I will take you through it;
It's a tough job, but someone's got to do it.

A BIT OF BACKGROUND

NEWPORT – DISAMBIGUATION

Newport, Newport. So good they name it twice. On the website of Traveline Cymru, that is. This is to distinguish it from Newport Pembrokeshire, Gloucestershire and Essex when faced with a multiple choice. It also avoids the vexed question of whether it is, at any given time, Newport Monmouthshire or Newport Gwent, I suppose.

This last question is discussed at length on the website thisisg-went.co.uk, though the irony of that seems to have escaped the enthusiastic contributors to it.

I am often asked where it really is, and how long it has been in Wales. This is what I have discovered.

THE LAND THAT TIME FORGOT

Once upon a time, O Best Beloved, there was a Land[1] that Time Forgot. It lay between two little rivers; the Rhymney and the Monnow and a big one, the Usk, ran down the middle. On the western side lived a Dragon and on the eastern side lived a Lion. In the high and far-off times the Dragon had ruled there, but when his territories were divided up into bite-sized chunks, so that Law and Order could be maintained[2], the drawer-uppers of the agreement forgot to include The Land. Oh, dear.

Some people assumed that, since it didn't officially belong to the Dragon any more, it must now belong to the Lion[3]. Others assumed that it still belonged to the Dragon and that the Lion had pinched it.

The Land rather liked being nobody's-in-particular. Its people went on being who they were and where they were, without being overly concerned with what they were. They were far too busy.

The Land prospered; it mined and it manufactured and soon it became the envy of the world. Its mighty Seaport traded merrily in coal and bananas and it spun between the Dragon and the Lion like a glitter-ball above a dancefloor, making rainbows on both sides of itself, until…

One day[4] the Lion woke up, stretched and walked to the edge of his domain and there, facing him, nose to nose, was the Dragon. The Dragon smiled.

Now Hear and Attend and Listen, O Best Beloved, for it had come about in this wise…

notes

1. The county of Monmouthshire, which came into existence in 1536 formed from several of the old Marcher Lordships.
2 1543 when it was omitted from the second Act of Union which established the Court of Great Session legal system in Wales.
3. The 1911 Encyclopædia Britannica unambiguously described the county as part of England, but notes that 'whenever an act [...] is intended to apply to [Wales] alone, then Wales is always coupled with Monmouthshire'.'
4. April Fool's Day 1974.

BEYOND A PERADVENTURE

On the 14th of March 1972 the Local Government Bill was being discussed in Parliament[1]. Mr Brynmor John (MP for Pontypridd) moved an amendment to the wording of one clause, suggesting that the words "In this section 'Wales' includes the administrative county of Monmouthshire and the county borough of Newport" be replaced by "For all purposes 'Wales' shall include… etc."

Mr George Thomas (MP for Cardiff West) supported his colleague with the words "I believe my honourable Friend is echoing the sentiments of the vast majority of Welsh people when we ask the Government to make clear beyond a peradventure that Monmouthshire belongs to the Principality."

Thus the wheels were set in motion. On the 20th July Mr George Thomas asked "has the Minister of State now announced that in future the argument about Monmouthshire being part of Wales is over and that this statement makes it clear that Monmouthshire is part of Wales for good and for ever?" and Mr Gibson-Watt replied "Yes".

The Member of Parliament for Manchester Ardwick, Mr. Gerald Kaufman, couldn't believe what he had just heard. "Am I to take it that an act of annexation of this magnitude is to be carried through a sparsely attended House of Commons on the nod at five minutes to midnight…? I wish to voice my protest."

His protest, however, fell on deaf ears and in due course the Local Government Bill was given Royal Assent and became an Act of Parliament which, in the words of George Thomas, "conferred respectability on the people of Monmouthshire".

And on April Fools' Day 1974, the good people of Newport, who had gone to bed the night before in their special, separate, slice of the

United Kingdom, woke up to find themselves in Wales. The dragon had stepped across the Usk. *Ilea iacta erat.*

notes

1. All quotations are taken directly from Hansard.

NEWPORT, COMPASSWISE

Writer proposes, publisher disposes. In that order. Just as I had assumed my work was coming to an end it was pointed out to me that, in order for this book to fit in with others in the series, I would have to present my findings in a cartographic context. I must place my subjects firmly in a recognised relationship to each other – north, south, east, west. I grasped the idea and sat down with a ruler and my wobbly map. And I found I couldn't do it.

I have never driven, not on real roads, not on my own. I am a simple person, a foot soldier. I live by right and left. North and south are abstract constructs created by minds far greater than mine. It's a sobering thought that, had I been working in the logistics department in the Age of Discovery, there'd be no America.

I saw what was appearing on the page and my heart sank. I was going to have to decide. I'm a poet; I don't do decisions. I felt my lower lip trembling in the way it used to do when I was at school. "Oh, Miss, I can't." The only thing that offered the slightest hope was the possibility of a truly creative excuse, which has always been one of my strengths. I started with the easy option: "Please Sir – the dog ate my homework..." At my feet, the dog shifted uneasily.

I opted for one last try after which I dissolved in tears of frustration:

Compasswise

Stop the computer! Isn't life a bitch?
I have encountered an almighty glitch:
To fit the pattern of what's gone before
I've got to carve the City into four.

I found it's not as easy as it looks.
I turned first to my main informant. Books.
Constituency-wise there's East and West
But no delineation of the rest.

There's no official north, no proper south
One is reliant upon word of mouth
Which will not do. I need to give the thing
A purely arbitrary quartering.

At first it seemed that there was nothing to it;
You find the centre, take a ruler – do it.
North must be upwards, south is down, as ever,
And east and west go straight across. That's clever.

But with a north-south vertical, the rest of it
Can only be either to east or west of it.
An east-west horizontal, by extension,
Can only show a north-or-south dimension.

So if an uppy-downy cross won't do
And side-to-sidey is a no-no too,
Since both present the place as what it ain't,
I need the intervention of a saint…

(prolonged interval of artistic snivelling, until…)

Look! Andrew has the answer! Bless the chap!
I'll scribe a saltire on the Newport map.
And then four equal slices will appear –
Northish, Southish, Eastish and Westish. Clear?

Indeed, by what felt like divine intervention, I had come upon a
workable solution. In my tearful extremity I had drawn an angry,
crossing out, bugger-it sort of X on my poor little map and could see
at once that it would answer my purpose. I rearranged it so the lines
intersected at the bus station, which is effectively the umbilicus of the
conurbation from the point of view of the non-driver and decided
that Central would apply to anywhere that could be walked to in
twenty-five minutes. Sorted. I warmed to my task. The dog relaxed.

NORTH

COMING DOWN THE VALLEY

In the old days, when I worked on the *Argus*, I lived nearer to Newport than I do now. I commuted on a 50cc motorcycle. That was stolen when I moved here, joyridden to Abertillery and burned on the mountain above Roseheyworth, while the thieves danced in the brief glow of its immolation. I am now reduced to the bus, my only choice being between Stagecoach and Glyn Williams. On the hour or the half-hour.

Glyn Williams' option has lately been sanctified by the wonderful Goldie Lookin Chain – arguably Newport's *jeunesse dorée* – who have implanted the suggestion that it is regularly used by clergy. Their design for living, they suggested, posed a threat to the fabric of society "even greater than that of havin' a stiffy while standin' in the middle of a Glyn William coach full of nuns" (*Manifesto*)

I myself have never seen persons of the cloth journeying on the X15, but on several occasions the man who sells the *Warcry* outside Blaina Co-op has snored his way back and forth a few seats away. Any form of overt arousal would simply pass him by as he zizzes stertorously in his private dream. He seems to have mastered the art of turning down the corner of it when forced to react or reply to a fellow-passenger, so that he can segue seamlessly back into it at the drop of an eyelid.

It's an hour and twenty minutes down the valley, during which one's mind is inclined to wander. Outside the primary school in Roseheyworth has appeared a strange sculpture that looks for all the world like a Wicker Man. With the new curricular emphasis on awareness of their Celtic roots I am not altogether surprised, although perhaps this is carrying things a little too far. It is comforting to realise that it is nowhere near big enough to accommodate a real man, though perhaps a small boy could be inserted without too much difficulty, if he were well greased...

Once there was once a tiny old lady who got on at Six Bells and sat beside me all the way to town. She fell asleep, too, but she was too small to reach my shoulder so she dozed against my upper arm and gradually slid onto my bosom, then down onto my lap. I woke her up when we arrived and she scampered off like a brisk squirrel. At first I thought that my leg felt cold because her warm little head had gone, but then I realised she had been dribbling on my thigh for almost an hour.

Over the years some constants have emerged. Very few journeys are achieved without an appearance of what I have come to call The

Soffryd Baby. Not that it always appears at Soffryd. It is not even a particular baby, a little individual. It is more of an archetype, a sign of the times hauled aboard in a buggy. Sometimes it sleeps. Sometimes it screams. Once, on a homeward journey, it hit out about itself with a free balloon from McDonalds like a malevolent jester, drooling and jeering, swiping with a pig's bladder at complacency and torpor. Like the Baby of Macon it is a wonder sent to teach us something about ourselves, though I am still at a loss to pin down its exact message. However, one of its manifestations produced the following half-educated guess:

The Baby's Hat

Some closet paedophile must have devised
This tortured pseudo-medieval shape,
Where two gross knitted twists rise either side
Of the bizarrely gift-wrapped fontanelle
To hang erratically at sad angles –
The shattered horns of a Levantine goat
Defeated in the rut. A feeble thread
Of ersatz swansdown burrows in and out
Of a row of ill-crafted openwork,
Emerging in apologetic tufts
Above the ears, like unsuccessful ferrets
Sniffing the wind, seeking the best way home.
Pink nylon ribbon mingles with the fluff
To form a background for the coup de grâce –
Fat plastic pearls, clinging like beads of sweat
Around the baby's flaky little forehead,
Artfully mirroring the beads of snot
Collected in its nostrils. I am moved
To snatch the child, to run away with it,
To hold it somewhere safe while I contrive
To conjure up a less abusive hat.

NEWBRIDGE

When I first started regular journeying up and down the valley I believed (perhaps erroneously) that the New Bridge was the one that carried the railway over the road. I loved going back and forth under it; it was newly painted with cheery childlike murals of a steam train full of waving people. I looked out for them and smiled.

They are probably still there; I think I can just see them but a fine growth of iron oxide has all but obscured them now. John Ruskin referred to rust as an 'ochreous stain', describing steel oxidization as a generative process rather than one of decay, as a quality of life, movement and metamorphosis. When I look at the bridge, though, and remember the train, I wonder about the place of natural processes in the matter of planning.

Here in Newbridge there was once a bank covered with hypericum – St. John's Wort – alongside the traffic lights that often held the bus for precious minutes beside the cataract of shimmering gold that would later impinge upon my inward eye like Wordsworth's daffs. I never wrote a poem about it, though, probably because I felt it had 'been done'. One day I passed and saw to my horror that the shrubs had been destroyed and their bodies covered with bark chippings. Then a wooden village appeared. It was painted in Pennsylvania Dutch shades of pink and blue and it was two-dimensional and artsy, like Portmeirion. I hated it with a passion and grieved for my fool's gold. But over the years the wooden village has cracked and faded and is slowly sinking into the chippings, which have rotted and succumbed to the tiny fungi that are still feasting on their remains. And the hypericum is creeping back. I am torn two ways. Part of me longs to see it in bloom again, as it used to be. The rest of me is willing it not to come out, not to give itself away, not to alert the authorities. Just in case.

But alas, it is not only the authorities who destroy Nature's spontaneous beauties. There is a special tree between Newbridge and Abercarn...

The Rude Tree

Some trick of growth had sculpted the beech roots
Into a piece of natural erotica.
Those in the know would point it out to friends

With a knowing wink. It was a landmark
Though not altogether easy to spot.
But in a day it changed; vandals had found it.
Painted it hastily in fishpaste pink.
Taken the natural joke and made it ugly.
Hammered it home hard, like the rusty spike
That they rammed into the apparent anus.
Drawn over the lines like a clumsy child
Who has lost interest in a spoiled picture:
"A kneeling dryad creeps, bare-arsed and beautiful
Into its sheltering tree..."

Coming down the home stretch. At the Tredegar Park roundabout the bus joins the A48 Cardiff Road, which was the A48 Newport Road when it left Cardiff. Past the Patent Office, the Statistics Office and the inside-out semi-conductor factory that was designed by Richard Rogers and still looks excitingly avant-garde. It is a crystallisation of his groundbreaking experimental work on the Pompidou Centre in Paris and precedes his creation of the Millennium Dome in London, so it could perhaps be perceived by some as the high point of his career.

On past the Catholic Church on Ebbw Bridge whose Jesus came down from the cross one night in the early nineties and was eventually re-crucified much later, when the builders got round to it. Then the small parade of shops which never seems to change (no, strike that, for fear of attracting the attention of some eavesdropping angel of mutability).

Here is Nando's, the place that has been offering haircuts forever, the betting shop and the Spar. Here is the Wai Wai Chinese takeaway – how should one pronounce it? It should surely be *why? why?* And here, forming the next block all by itself is the low, flat, sad-faced building where I spent most of my first years in Newport; the headquarters of the *South Wales Argus*.

From here it's a straight whizz into town. Or a crawl if

it's the rush hour. Past the post office in the breeze-block shed, the impressive gates and green overhang of Belle Vue Park, the Royal Gwent, red and huge and terrifying, with the dear little GUM clinic, ivy-clad, all by itself on the periphery. The Newport Denture Laboratory (ah, my time will come).

The last chance to jump ship before town is the big grassy roundabout with the smart lavvies and the Merchant Navy memorial. When I was with the *Argus* it was always known as Gilligan's Island because of the happy coincidence of the adjacent family-owned fish shop and the cult Sixties sitcom. Although both these have disappeared into history and the island is now officially called Mariner's Green, the old name still lingers on the lips of the locals. From here you get a good view of one of the best buildings in Newport; the hilarious Gwent Police Headquarters that looks as if it is made of Lego, precise and perfect with all the patterns built in. It is a pleasing edifice that always makes me grin, leading to silly visions of cylindrical officers with little pink ball-heads and really smiley faces. Yeah. As if...

Then the chicken-and-chippies, the tat shop, the Private Shop with the blacked-out windows and one quick squinny up Commercial Street before the bus swings right and follows Kingsway, trundling between the Dolman Theatre and the Newport Centre to fall exhausted into Bay Seven of the sainted Bus Station.

CAERLEON

Start again at the bus station, stand 25. Any bus with a 2 on it, be it 2a, b, c, d, e or x, will get you to Caerleon. So will the maverick 7d, but I don't quite trust it; you never know with sevens. Set aside a whole day for Caerleon; it's worth it.

Until the nineteenth century, Caerleon was the major port on the Usk. At one time it boasted forty-one different venues where intoxicating liquor could be had – although that's cheating a bit since one of them was the Catholic Church and I don't think you can count Communion wine unless you are 'of the fold', so to speak. It still has a hostelry or two, together with a wonderful little shopping precinct called the Ffwrrm, and on a hill above the town is one of the campuses of the University of Wales, Newport. It is also claimed as the location of the Celtic Manor Resort, which is hosting the Ryder Cup in 2010, but there is a good deal of controversy about this. It has been rumoured that the management would do just about anything to get the word 'Newport' out of its postal address. However, I think its location overlooking the Coldra roundabout is a bit suspect post-codally as far as Caerleon is concerned.

Caerleon, though, has other claims to celebrity. There are questions a visitor must ask:

WAS IT CAMELOT?

In 830AD Nennius wrote *Historia Brittonum*. Nennius was a Welsh monk who lived in Bangor and as a historian he was a very good monk indeed. His book was a wonderful collection of ripping yarns mainly about mythical Celtic heroes. The genealogy didn't stand up to scrutiny and Nennius never let the doubtful veracity of his sources stand in the way of his narrative. He confesses, bless him, in an apologetic preface, 'I have made a heap of all that I could find'. Oh, dear reader – I know the feeling.

The things that found their way into his heap were now-lost fifth century manuscripts and round-the-fire tales of Welsh folklore. He washed them all together and the colours ran, but the result was not a complete waste. *Historia Brittonum* records Caerleon as one of Britain's thirty-three cities and contains the first written reference to Arthur, whom he describes as a warrior who united the Britons in their fight against the Saxons. It also includes a list of Arthur's battles one of which took place at 'The City of the Legion'. This could well be Caerleon, whose Welsh name means 'Fortress Of The Legion'. Caerleon is known to have had a large civilian population living immediately outside the fortress walls so it would have qualified as a city, the criteria of the time being more relaxed in these matters.

Nennius himself is a hard chap to pin down. I have tried. The different Latin manuscripts of Nennius vary so widely that it's impossible to establish a standard text. It looks as though every scribe who copied the work had doubts about it and corrected and added to it in an attempt to improve it. Nowadays it seems that many scholars believe that Nennius did not, in fact, write Nennius. It's starting to get deep now, like Shakespeare and Bacon and Marlowe – best not go there – but you can't help wondering what any anonymous author stood to gain from posing as an ignorant Welsh monk.

Whole academic careers have been built on interpreting the Arthurian material in Nennius and for every version of the Latin there are ten times as many English translations. You pays your money and you takes your choice.

You may not think much of Nennius but Geoffrey of Monmouth is generally regarded as having a more informed view. Possibly from his own backyard. Monmouth is, after all, but a cockstride from Caerleon, and he must have been impressed by the splendid Roman remains which we know existed then. In his work *Historia Regum Britanniae* (History of the Kings of Britain) he described how Arthur held court at the 'City of the Legion'. He may have pinched the name from Nennius, but he goes on to make it quite clear that he's talking about Caerleon:

> When the feast of Whitsuntide began to draw near, Arthur, who was quite overjoyed by his great success, made up his mind to hold a plenary court at that season, wearing the crown of the kingdom on his head. He decided too, to summon to this feast the leaders who owed him homage, so that he could celebrate Whitsun with greater reverence and renew the closest pacts of peace with his chieftains. He explained to the members of his court what he was proposing to do and accepted their advice that he should carry out his plan in The City Of The Legion. Situated as it is in Morgannwg, on the River Usk, not far from the Severn Sea, in a most pleasant position, and being richer in material wealth than other townships, this city was eminently suitable for such a ceremony. The river which I have named flowed by it on one side, and up this the kings and princes who were to come from across the sea could be carried in a fleet of ships. On the other side, which was flanked by meadows and wooded groves, they had adorned the city with royal palaces, and by the gold-painted gables of its roofs it was a match for Rome.

According to Geoffrey, Caerleon was a place of great significance even before Arthur. It had an archbishop who was clearly a person of importance because it was his job to crown ings. He tells us:

> After the death of Uther Pendragon, the leaders of the Britons assembled from their various provinces in the town of Silchester and there suggested to Dubricius, the archbishop of the City Of The Legions,

that as their King he should crown Arthur, son of Uther. He called the other bishops to him and bestowed the crown of the kingdom upon Arthur. Arthur was a young man only fifteen years old...

Caerleon was obviously a splendid place and it was no surprise that Arthur should have held his court there. What a pity Geoffrey didn't go the whole way and call it Camelot.

In fact, Camelot was invented by the French poet Chrétien de Troyes, writing fifty years later. But he must have read Geoffrey and surely Geoffrey's Caerleon was his inspiration. I choose to believe so and I invite you to join me. If you do, you'll be in good company, because it was to Caerleon that Tennyson turned when he was writing *Idylls of the King* in 1856. He lodged in the Hanbury Arms, which he used as a touring base for tramping the countryside and assimilating the Arthurian vibes. He also spent much time staring out of the pub window at the up-and-down Usk. Visitors can still sit in 'Tennyson's Window' and dream up stories like that. Or this.

To Camelot

Yobs untie the cabin cruiser
Left to rot beside the river,
Drag her down and turn her over,
Push her out onto the water
   Just to see if she will float.
Reeboks crushing frosty sedges
All along the water's edges,
Hurling missiles from the bridges
   At the dented, dying boat.

First she proudly breasts the current,
Rides the river, heir apparent
To the beauty of the torrent,
Off to face her final moment
   Elemental and alone.
But the yobs continue throwing,
Conscious of their power, knowing
They can still control her going –
   One more swearword, one more stone!

Laughing with the joy of wrecking;
Shattered screen and splintered decking.
Listing, lurching, bobbing, jinking,
Now she founders, now she's sinking –
   Yeah! Titanic! Gissa shot!
Little bits of broken mirror
Catch the sunset on the river
Where the song goes on forever
   All the way to Camelot.

OR IS IT ROME?

I found the following profound observation when I looked up
Caerleon on the Internet:

> **Caerleon is an enormously interesting place to anyone with an
> interest, however small, in Roman history.**

There is no answer to that.

II Augusta was one of the four Roman legions, each of around six
thousand men, plus auxiliaries, which invaded Britain in AD 43. The
Legion was named after the Emperor Augustus, whose birthsign,
Capricorn, was the symbol on their standard. They were first based
in the South West in a camp they built at Exeter - which they named
Isca Dumnoniorum. This was the base from which they subdued and
civilised the local tribesmen,
the Dumnonii.

When they were redeployed
to Wales to deal with the
powerful Silures, they established a new base at Caerleon
in AD 75. They called this one
Isca Silurum (go figure!). The
site was chosen as it was about
as far inland as the Roman
ships could bring supplies. It
enjoyed the same relationship
with the Usk as had the other
Isca with the Exe.

The Legion pulled out of Caerleon some time around AD 290. Before they left, they demolished the main buildings. The thrifty Normans, looking for likely materials for the upgrading of the area – as you or I might peer surreptitiously into a skip – found all sorts of bits and pieces that were too good to waste. The earliest part of the existing St Woolos Cathedral, the entrance chapel, has a lovely arch made of purloined pillars from the remains of Isca Silurum.

Troops from Caerleon were posted to many parts of the country. Some were responsible for building sections of Hadrian's Wall. Later legionaries probably did not thank them for it.

A Cold Night on the Wall

Miles Romanus sum; arma virumque cano.
It's going to be a cold night on the wall –
The sky's too high; there are too many stars
And all my leather gear is damp and dull.
Rufus has ten more minutes. Let him come
And get me when it's time. Let his dog-breath
Crisp on his beard until his watch is up.
I'll stay here in the washhouse underneath
The atrium. There's still a drop of wine
That's bought and paid-for. I shall see it off;
Let Rufus come and get me when it's time.
Bugger Brigantia! I've had enough
Of bloody Celts.
    The fuddle-headed soldier
Pokes with his short-sword at the wash-house floor
Methodically winkling-out and flicking
The little tesserae: one, two, three, four…
Rome was not built in a day. Brutus sits
Meticulously picking it to bits.

But it's surprising how many of those bits are still to be found, especially since a whole culture of excavation and conjecture has arisen in their places of origin.

Here in Caerleon the conservationists have enshrined the bits in an exemplary setting. What's left of the baths, the barracks, the kitchens, the latrines are all to be found around the town. The rest of the stuff, tiles, pots, jewellery, glassware, human remains and inhuman detritus, is all housed in the Legionary Museum, eked out by reconstructions of best-guesses and informed extrapolations. I love it all.

It was there that I watched one of the staff members, a tired, middle-aged woman in a straight skirt and ill-fitting shoes, recreate the life of a legionary soldier for a mixed group of children and adults who watched and listened, fascinated. The poor woman must have done hundreds of these presentations, putting on the helmet and brandishing the *pilum*, the *gladius* and the *pugio*. Showing the sponge-on-a-stick that they used for wiping their backsides (pause for giggles) and explaining the purpose of the surprisingly sophisticated surgical instruments, but she made it come alive, fresh and new. I admired her skill, but recognised a kindred spirit. Here was another lover of this amazing civilisation whose influence crawls under the skin like scabies and itches unexpectedly at inopportune moments.

Defixio

From a lead curse tablet left at the
shrine to Nemesis in Isca Silurum

Last night I lay with him I love.
We did the thing not spoken of.
It ended well, but as he came
He whispered someone else's name.
I love my love. I always will.
I do not seek to do him ill,
Nor do I wish the woman harm
Beyond the limits of this charm:
Oh, Eros, if this once I may
Prefer you over Agapé,
Be there when next he is with her
And in extremis, as it were.
Then, as he sighs in ecstasy,
Contrive to make him mention me.

CAERLEON COLLEGE

In the late nineties, when he was already terminally ill, my husband Philip enrolled for a degree course at Caerleon College. Because he was unable to move far without a wheelchair and occasionally needed nursing care at short notice, I was included in the placement as his carer. We became students again together and the relationship between the Romans and the Celts was our area of special study. It was a happy time despite the extraordinary circumstances and I was glad of the chance to study, albeit unofficially, a subject so close to my heart.

And I learned a lot at Caerleon. I loved every minute and tiptoed with bated breath into many areas of archaeology that had hitherto been mysteries to me. Carbon dating, for instance, and the importance of *c-transformation*. I had a bit of trouble getting to grips with that. Apparently when one finds certain substances during an investigation, especially the examination of 'grave-goods', the trained mind can extrapolate backwards to determine what they had been heretofore. I assumed that this would go on into the future and that new substances would lay down their own rules for the process.

c-transformation

Full six feet deep thy father lies
Of his bones are carbons made
Cheap shoes and polyester ties
Archaeologists upgrade
Till they suffer a c-change
Into something rich and strange.
Hourly they argue his home and habit
Hark! Now I hear them…*rabbit, rabbit…*

Rabbits appeared often during lectures. Sometimes the speaker would leave us behind a bit and the rabbit became an acknowledgement of the occasional obscurity employed by experts who find themselves preaching to the genuinely unconverted. If Philip felt he was losing his grasp of an argument, he would doodle a rabbit on the edge of his notepad and call my attention to it with a flourish of his eyebrows. He did this during a lecture on 'Celticity' and I replied with a rabbit of my own and a verse to sum up where we'd got to:

This *(right)* is a rabbit
from Rennes,
Demonstrably Celtic (La
Tène)
He has a treskele
Tattooed on his belly
Which dates him to
round about then.

This is a rabbit from Rennes
Demonstrably Celtic (la Tène)
He had a treskele
Tattooed on his belly
Which dates him to round about then

But we did take the studies seriously and we didn't miss a single one of the special lectures right up to the day Philip died. However, things were not always easy for a disabled student and a supernumerary carer. One meeting in particular proved especially problematic.

Philip's wheelchair was placed in the front row and I perched on a desk beside him. It was hellish hot and the edge of the desk threatened to cut off the blood supply to my lower legs. We were attending a lecture entitled 'Roman Invasion: Conflict or Consensus?' I kept repeating it in my head and playing it surreptitiously on the desk with the tips of my fingers; the sound of it pleased me hugely, echoing as it did the hendecasyllabic music in the poetry of Catullus. I wondered if this was deliberate. I rather hoped so, but nobody else mentioned it and I didn't dare ask, just in case. I hid behind my role of carer, listening hard for all I was worth. That, it transpired, was all either of us could do, as the visiting academic stood with his back to us, effectively obscuring the flipchart. In an attempt to take my mind off my deadening legs, I made notes, recreating the picture that was being drawn by the gesticulating lecturer…

Roman Invasion: Conflict or Consensus?

…Here comes Claudius, sailing up the Solent
(Not too fast on account of the elephants)
All dressed up in his people-pleasing purple
Out on deck with the shiny-looking soldiers
Standing straight as his gammy leg will let him,
Face all stretched with the effort of his trying
Not to laugh at the acrobatic pirates…

I loved the acrobatic pirates. The lecturer insisted that they were germane to his argument for a degree of collaboration between the invading forces and the would-be client kings. When I later got a look at one of the other students' notes, I glumly observed that they were actually "Atrebatic pilots". But by then it was too late.

After Philip's death I came alone to Caerleon to scatter a handful of his ashes.

The Amphitheatre at Caerleon

Appropriate? I thought so. We were both
Enthralled by Rome. You were a businessman,
I was a farmer. We were both concerned
With thoughts of empire and responsibility.
This brought you, at the end, to study here:
Romano-Celtic archaeology.
You fell half way to your Master's degree
Like a defeated gladiator. Requies.
And here was where I found the broken sign –
This way to the Roman Baths; white on brown
As is deemed meet for ancient monuments.
It had been snapped off where it joined the post.
I found it hidden in some little bushes
And asked the warden if he wanted it:
No, you can have it, love. It can't be mended.
It's cast you see, that means you can't weld it.
All you can do is make another one.
If you can find the mould. And if there's time…

And on my last visit to Caerleon it was still there. Not the sign, I mean, but the broken stump on the post. The sign itself is in my garden. Cherished.

CELTIC MANOR

Well, what a daft name, I thought when I first heard it. A contradiction in terms if ever I heard one. One thing Celts didn't have was manors. They represented an entirely different lifestyle. I tried to be smug and dismissive, but without success. It kept cropping up in conversation.

I have heard so much about the place. For ages people have been thrusting it under my nose as one of the rare positives in an otherwise sorry scenario. "Ryder Cup", they keep telling me. "Two thousand and ten". And although it took me a while to realise that this trophy was for golf and not tennis, as I had heretofore supposed, I was forced to admit that it was an impressive coup. Ryder Cup, eh? *Wow!*

And then the appearance of its restaurant as a new entry in the *Good Food Guide*. Even more impressive. But most of all, the story of the place is bound up in that of its creator, Sir Terry Matthews, Wales's first official billionaire. He made it; it is his.

So what is it then, this Celtic Manor? Its own website describes it as "a five-star resort at the gateway to Wales". More prosaic sources describe it as a modern 400-bedroom hotel set in 1,400 acres with in spitting distance of the M4 with all the leisure and health club facilities a well-heeled traveller could shake a *Rough Guide* at. I didn't like the sound of it at all. Not my kind of thing. Its founder, though, sounded an interesting sort of chap.

Terry Matthews didn't sound like the sort of young man who could be described as "to the manor born". But he was. In 1943 he was safely delivered in the Manor House maternity home in Newport, once the mansion of a steel magnate.

A Valleys boy, from Newbridge, home of the rusty bridge and the rude tree, he studied engineering at Swansea and started work an apprentice with BT. He was in Canada on holiday in 1969 when he was offered a job and stayed there. In 1972 he founded the Mitel Corporation, which I am told, designed and manufactured "high

tech voice communication systems". I think they mean telephones. In 1985, he sold it to BT and started a new communications company – which he called Newbridge Networks, even though it was located in Canada. It was bought by a French company in 2000 for almost £5 billion.

He was knighted in 2001, which caused a wee diplomatic riftette. The Canadian Prime Minister phoned up Tony Blair to express his displeasure. Terry Matthews, he said, was Canadian and his acceptance of a foreign honour breached national protocol. *Tant pis.* Terry Matthews is a Welsh National Hero. Celtic Manor is the largest-ever private investment in the British hospitality industry. And the restaurant, Owens, and the health and fitness suite, Dylans, are named after two of his sons. No apostrophes, noted the

copy-editor in me, but you can't have everything.

It was on a return visit to Wales that he spotted the old maternity home, boarded up and slithering into decay. He bought it and did it up and it became the first Celtic Manor in 1982, winning the Egon Ronay award for best hotel in Wales for five consecutive years. It's still operating as a separate hotel and I found it described as follows: *This former Victorian mansion is a beautiful sandstone building with the original Georgian windows...* hold it! That can't be right. Not unless the steel magnate was into architectural salvage, which I doubt... *Wood panelled walls and a sweeping wooden staircase...ornate ceiling plasterwork is complemented with the traditional English (sic) style country interior.*

What a pity, I thought, as I stood in the courtyard in front of it, that no mention is made of the huge, modern, single-storey, flat-roofed red-brick extension that has been tacked onto the front of it. Long and low with lots of glass, it looks for all the world like a state-of-the-art accident and emergency department, making the place look more like a hospital than it ever did when it was a maternity home.

The Manor, as it is now called is on the right as you walk up the hill towards the main hotel. I took a detour for a look at it on my way to investigate the Celtic Manor Resort.

A few days earlier I had telephoned to ask how to get there by bus. A voice said "where may I direct your call?" It was pure sitcom and I was for a moment tempted to make a reply that would have seriously dented my image as a gentlewoman. When I confided the nature of my need, I was put through to 'Concierge' who introduced himself as Paul. He told me that the best way was to catch the Stagecoach Chepstow bus and ask to be put off at Celtic Manor.

There were city buses, green-and-cream, which went to a stop called Royal Oak, but it was a longer walk... Somehow I had not expected to be so well instructed. I asked where I might have lunch and was told there were three choices – Merlins Bar, The Olive Tree and the Lodge out on the golf course, at all of which I would be welcome, with no need to book.

I had terrible memories of a golf club in Dorset where I had been taken by a couple I didn't know well, friends of my late husband. There was a rule, I was told. No jeans. I put on a skirt, though I felt uncomfortable in it, but I had no alternative to my denim jacket. The lady eyed it nervously all the way to the door, then, as we entered, she whipped it off my shoulders in one fluid motion and twiddled it inside out like a practised prestidigitator before shiftily smuggling an armful of shiny lining past the gorgon on duty in the cloakroom. I asked warily about dress code at Celtic Manor. Paul laughed.

The chip on my shoulder shrunk a little, but I noticed that he had not mentioned the star restaurant, Owens, and I immediately assumed that this was because it was not for the likes of those who had to travel by bus. It later transpired that it was simply not an option for lunch because it only opens for dinner.

Mind you, none of them were an option that day, since I was far too broke to buy so much as a burger. But I strode up the tree-lined avenue in fine style, stopping only to admire a magnificent oak half way to the top. A Turkey Oak. *Quercus Cerris*. Introduced in the eighteenth century. A gentleman's tree, a parkland tree. No use for timber... And there I went again – a trendy-lefty pseudo-intellectual, envious of privilege. I

helped myself to a pocketful of acorns as a souvenir of the Celtic Manor Resort, which was as yet invisible. A slight bend in the road and there it was, or rather one corner of it, peeping out from yet more wonderful mature trees.

It is huge. It looks like an enormous casino. To get a picture of it I had to walk backwards onto the golf course and even then I couldn't quite get it all in. I saw a man with the longest squeegee in the world wiping at the downstairs windows; I noticed that the edges of the verges opposite the building had been lovingly re-seeded. Then I went for a walk.

There were golf courses. Of course. But I have only played golf once in the last twenty years and that was in Tavistock with the poet Matthew Sweeney, who explained the

rules to me a little at a time, so that every thing I thought I'd just done right was almost immediately proved wrong. It was great fun. But apart from the courses, there were woods. Trees that have been there far longer than the hotel. Trees that are cherished and respected. Here and there were little dells with natural streams in them, full of brambles, untidy and untouched. Perhaps they were 'hazards' for golfers, but not to the birds, who clearly loved them. Not to the wildflowers and the fungi.

Oh, sure – the greens were manicured to a velvety turf, the Rorschach bunkers raked to impossible perfection but the rough bits, the wooded corners, the deep, dark, safe coverts were a joy. I explored eagerly, making one gleeful discovery after another. Little golf carts came and went in the distance. I was reminded of my old life in Yorkshire, where the working shepherds shared the moors with the gentry, who nurtured the game and sold the shooting rights. As far as overall management was concerned, it transpired that what was good for the grouse was good for the sheep and the two enterprises complemented each other, while keeping up the old rivalries for the sake of appearance and tradition. Something of the sort was happening here and the thought made me happy.

I had wandered out onto an open area to see how far I could see. The sky, which had been a sort of dull slate grey turned to the ugly yellow of a day-old bruise. A rumble of thunder changed the channel and the birds stopped singing. Within minutes a deluge began and I ran for cover. I negotiated a huge and unusually user-friendly revolving door and found myself, wet and dishevelled, in the foyer of the

Celtic Manor Resort. On either side of a comfortable seating area were two huge marble pillars and around each was coiled a mighty wooden dragon. I went to reception to ask if I could take a photograph of them. I promised I would not inconvenience the patrons. I was sure they'd say no.

They said yes. The pleasant girl told me conspiratorially that one of the dragons was a boy and one was a girl and that I could take as many photographs as I liked. I did, wandering round seeing and feeling and thinking.

The décor was opulent but understated (apart from the dragons). It put me in mind of a set for a *Poirot* film. In a corner by the door a red pillar box stood ready for letters. There were sculptures and paintings most of which I found pleasing. One witty concession to *nouveau richesse* that amused me hugely was the giant Rolex wall-clock. It was when I went to get a photograph of it that I sensed that I had walked up a wide gentle slope to find the ideal viewpoint. I continued uphill into Merlins Bar. It took me a while to realise that this was perfect, integrated disabled access. The same discreet slopes were apparent elsewhere. I now understood that this was what had been so unusual about the revolving door – I could have easily got in with a wheelchair or a baby-buggy. All the doorways seemed more generous than usual and in the loo there was good light and wonderful chrome cross-head taps with ceramic centres – Hot and Cold. For some reason this delighted me.

There were not many patrons in evidence. I said hello to an American lady in a bright red jumper who was concerned, but not very, about her husband who was out on the golf course "in this" –

she indicated the storm, about which I had quite forgotten. I felt safe.

I sat on a comfortable chair at a glass-topped table, making notes. A hotel employee passed and caught my eye with a dazzling smile. How nice, I thought, then realised that his smile had simply mirrored my own. I felt relaxed and unthreatened. Pity I wouldn't get to see Owens unpossessive restaurant, but – never mind. I remembered something I had read about Owen Matthews in a Canadian business magazine. He is now a tycoon himself, owner and founder of New Heights Software Corporation, but at one time he had wanted to be a writer. I hoped he finds ways of making himself time to do it, between deals. It's a fine thing, being a writer. I looked at the notebook on the table and wished Owen well.

It had stopped raining. The smell of wet trees and the adventure of wet sloping tarmac enlivened my journey back to the bus stop, at which a 74 magically appeared within minutes. I spent those minutes in pleasant recollection. I had gone there with a bad heart, hoping to find targets to shoot at; instead I felt as if I had just been somewhere nice, and was feeling the benefit.

ANOTHER WAY OF COMING IN FROM THE NORTH

In the days of Newport's industrial greatness, there was another way of getting there that didn't involve roads at all. A system of canals was built to carry coal and iron to Newport Docks and played a significant part in the rapid expansion of the town. The Monmouthshire Canal was completed in 1799 and consisted of two branches, one to Pontnewynydd in the Eastern Valley and one to Crumlin in the Western Valley. In 1812 it was joined, literally, at Pontymoile by the Brecknock and Abergavenny Canal. The later canal starts in Brecon and thirty-three miles remain navigable. It is being shifted bodily out of the way of the widening Heads of the Valleys Road at the moment. The whole network is now known collectively as the Monmouthshire and Brecon Canal – or the 'Mons and Breck' to the cognoscenti.

The old Monmouthshire Canal, here and there weedy, here and there waterless, here and there triumphantly, landlockedly navigable, still joins Newport to the Valleys, though it doesn't quite go all the way any more. Neither does it start exactly where it used to. When the western arm of the canal was completed in 1799, it came up the valley by means of thirty-two locks as far as the terminal basin at Crumlin; it doesn't any more. Here's why.

One hundred and twenty three years to the day before the hi-jacked planes hit the Twin Towers, another explosion tore through a community not far from where I sit. At approximately 12.15pm on the 11th September 1878 the people of Abercarn heard an ominous underground rumbling, followed by the sound of the colliery steam whistle screaming for help. The disaster at the Prince of Wales Colliery was one of the worst in the history of the South Wales Coalfield. When that day began three hundred and twenty-five men and boys were working underground and when it ended two hundred and sixty-eight of them were dead.

Rescue teams were lowered into the pit to be confronted by smoke, fires and an insidious build-up of toxic gases. A man by the name of John Harris was awarded a gold Albert Medal for his actions on that day. He went down the pit with one of the rescue teams but the cage got stuck in the damaged shaft. He climbed out of the cage and shinnied down one of the guide ropes to the bottom, where he stayed for several hours until he was convinced that there was nobody left alive.

I hope he never, ever doubted that in later years. You see, because of the raging underground fires and the likelihood of further explo-sions, the rescue teams were recalled to the surface and the colliery manager, on the advice of mines inspectors, took the unenviable decision to flood the mine with water from the nearby canal. It took two months and thirty-five million gallons of water before the authorities were satisfied that the fires had been extinguished. The water then had to be pumped out before the grim task of removing the bodies could begin. Not all the dead were recovered; some were left entombed. A skeleton was found some twenty-seven years later, still in pit clothes and boots, and there was no way of telling how he had died.

So the canal stops suddenly, for no apparent reason, just north of Pontywaun. It no longer passes through Abercarn to Crumlin. And now you know why.

The Monmouthshire Canal Company also built a series of tramways (or dramroads as they are called locally) so that goods could be hauled on rails into Newport. They were converted to standard gauge railways in 1855, when a passenger service was begun and the whole network was handed over to Great Western Railways in 1875.

The Monmouthshire Canal Company with its canal and tramroads was responsible for the growth of Newport, which became the third largest coal port in Britain. In 1796 the Company shipped 3,500 tons of coal from its wharves on the River Usk. By 1809 this had grown to 150,000 tons. However, due to competition from roads and railways most commercial traffic had ceased by 1930 and the canal in Newport fell into a state of neglect with large sections becoming unnavigable and many locks unusable.

And here's where the cognoscenti come in. The water-gipsies and eco-freaks, the wannabe boaties and the loony aficionados have taken the waterway to their hearts, God bless them and prosper their work. They have formed pressure groups. They have convinced councils and tourist organisations and it is being restored, little by little. No, you still can't navigate the full length of it any more, though it is intended that in the foreseeable future you will be able to. What you can do, though, apart from a few missing bits, is walk along the towpath all the way to Newport.

My dog Otis and I made it our business to walk down the Crumlin arm to Newport to see how they're getting on. We started at what is now the beginning of it, at the foot of the approach road to Cwmcarn Forest Drive, and set off down a somewhat clinical path from the wall which marks the end of the canal. Oddly, the water doesn't come quite as far as the wall; it is stopped a few yards short of it by a rough-and-ready dam of the sort that children make as a whole-holiday project on a local stream. A new, shiny bin for dogs' doings declared the place fit for canine exploration and we set off, equipped with the necessary trappings of good citizenry so as to react appropriately should Otis be taken short (a knocking bet).

This is the most recently restored section of the canal. A navigable mile and half from the slipway by the Cwmcarn Spiritualist Church to a new and unfinished-looking 'Whysom Wharf' whose pristine sign looks out of place alongside the old bridge where the stretch ends abruptly in another brick wall.

This is pleasant walking, but a little eerie. The water is cloudy, the edges deep and the banks high, the neoprene lining still visible above the water. After an initial gallop down the slipway for a joyous wallow and a bellyful of canal, Otis was unable to reach it again, despite leaning his whole furry length down the bank in an effort to do so. The trees were in full leaf, the sunlight dappling the water. Not a fish stirred. It looked like a new-made pond waiting for something to happen. Not much was going on in in the water, but on the towpath the occasional fiendishly-fast bicycle threatened to hurl me into it for a better look.

I am not the world's straightest walker at the best of times and do not have the ears of a bat. Anything that approaches silently from the rear will be ignored. All those wildlife films about the lone leopard and the Thomson's Gazelle will have told you how it works and the paintings of *le douanier* Rousseau will show you how it ends. Otis was doing something interesting and I was attempting to catch him on camera. I activated the zoom lens and stepped back to get the perfect angle, only to collide with a cyclist who had been about to overtake me on the left.

"Why the hell," he enquired with commendable restraint, "don't you look where you're going?" "I was," I replied with similar affability, "in order to have known you were there I'd have had to have been looking where I'd been." Several other cyclists whizzed by from behind during the walk, skimming past either shoulder with heartstopping suddenness. No reason they shouldn't have been there; it's a designated cycle path and I gather a bell is no longer compulsory, but whatever happened to the polite 'excuse me', the strategic clearing of the throat or even the exasperated 'Achtung!' My own bicycle has a bell that goes "ding-dong" – but then it also has a skirt-guard and a wicker basket. These state-of-the-art veloci-pedes seem at odds with the pace of the canal, yet if they weren't there the tourism lobby would have fewer cards to play. And Otis seemed to have no problem with them.

One of the strange things about being on the canal is the way the rest of the world disappears. Not in the romantic sense of withdrawing to allow poetic contemplation; it just is no longer there. As we walked that first stretch of canal, I soon lost all track of where we were in relation to the places I knew were along the road.

Even a map wouldn't have helped, because there are no landmarks that relate to them. I could hear a small and not very busy road way down to my right and left, across the water, was a green wooded hillside. I could have been anywhere.

Where the canal ended, two ducks dabbled halfheartedly and watched us with half an eye as we went up into sunlight and civilisation. A man and a dog came towards us. At the risk of being thought daft, I asked "Where am I?" He told me I was in Fernlea. "Where's the canal?" He pointed across a main road. And sure enough there was another wall, from which the canal twinkled on in the direction of Risca.

But what a difference. This bit had been restored some time ago and the water was brown but clear. Small fish were visible and a heron flew off as we approached. Natural erosion and lateral accumulation had made little gritty beaches and when Otis ran joyfully down onto one of them he was encircled by electric-blue damselflies as he snapped at the water-boatmen on the surface. There was a family of busy moorhens and here and there great rafts of waterlilies thrumming with insects. For a while the towpath ran alongside the gardens of houses, each of which had created steps up to it and a gate that opened onto it. Here the canal is clearly a treasured amenity. And quite right, too.

Through a break in the houses I could make out Risca, way, way below, and the canal curved round the side of the valley, through the less picturesque Ty Sign Estate. I have always been a little afraid of Ty Sign. In the days when I drove home on my little motorcycle in late summer, I would come round the bend into Tredegar Street and the evening sun would strike the all the windows on the estate at once. This gave it the appearance of gleaming cohorts, all purple and gold, standing poised with polished shields, waiting for the signal to descend on Risca like a wolf on the fold. I knew that if they did I'd never get out in time, especially since my 50ccs couldn't really exceed 30mph. I acknowledged the influence of Byron, but nonetheless I sensed malevolence.

Now, here we were, up among the Assyrians themselves. To cheer myself up as we followed the canal past the sleeping soldiers, I thought of a less terrifying poem.

> Journey with us, the infant children of Ty Sign,
> Along the gravelly path beside the canal.
> One lonely duck on the rippling muddy water, swimming
> Past our school with children working very hard at writing, sums
>   and painting.
> Past the houses where families live, under the busy road with
>   speeding cars,
> And on towards the stoney bridge and the church.
> We're lucky to have the changing canal to look at through the
>   seasons.
> Come on!

(Part of a long poem composed for National Poetry Day 2004 by all the schoolchildren of Caerphilly County Borough. This bit was by Ty Sign Infants, bless them).

From here the canal goes on through Rogerstone and enters a wooded cutting which takes it from the Western to the Eastern Valley. Even the towpath changes sides before the Fourteen Locks at High Cross. These locks were built to carry the canal down 168 feet in less than 900 yards, using a series of pounds and ponds to conserve as much water as possible. Halfway up the flight one of the locks, known as 'the sea lock' was built wide at the top to allow boats to pass. In the seventies there were plans to fill the locks in and leave them at just a few inches depth for safety and the side ponds were to be converted into paddling pools. They were saved when Newport Council took over the running of the district in 1974. They smartened the place up, turning it into a park complete with a canal visitor centre. Part of me resents the souvenirs and sweeties, but it's a small price to pay for the preservation of something so precious. It is here that the most recent piece of restoration has been accomplished. The Canal Trust now run hour-long trips through their newly-opened lock.

After Fourteen Locks, a stretch with five single locks takes the canal round the bottom of Allt Yr Yn and into the shadow of the M4, which is never out of earshot from here to the junction with the Eastern branch at Malpas. Here we emerge like Startrekkers onto an alien planet, disoriented and a little afraid as the traffic not grown-up enough for the motorway hurtles with apparently unnecessary speed towards Cwmbran. It's life, Captain – but not as we know it.

THE CIVIC

Newport's Civic Centre – 'The Civic' as it known in the city – is an undeniably impressive building. It dominates the skyscape as you enter Newport by train and if you've woken up suddenly it sets your mind at rest as to where you are if you are in an aisle seat and unable to see the mud. There is only one of it and nobody else has got one. It is a huge white monument to the sunset of Art Deco. Its mighty clock-tower, just a tad too tall in proportion to the rest of the building, is prevented from looking pompous by the addition of a little black beret on the top, like a French Johnny-onions.

The Civic was commissioned by the then Newport Corporation in 1936 and an open competition was held for its design. T. Cecil Howitt, of Nottingham, was selected for the project. I, for one, am extremely pleased. King George VI visited Newport and cut the first sod of the project in 1937, but it was a long time in the building. Work was brought to a halt by the war and it was opened for business, albeit unfinished, in 1940.

Work began again in the fifties, and on the 10th September 1963 the Borough Council voted to complete the building in accordance with the original design. The clock-tower was approved at a cost of £126,900 (peanuts by today's standards) despite a poll of 8,734 signatures in which the public voted forty to one against. When I think of what happened to so many cities in the sixties, how Bristol and Plymouth were disfigured by huge ugly lumps of 'modernity' which are only now being excised like warts from their faces, I salute the brave Council who kept faith with one man's original vision.

Close up, The Civic is wide and inviting with broad steps and a feel of substance and comfortable efficiency, like an old-fashioned policeman. On my first visit I was especially struck by the heavy smell of hyacinths that hung in the still air between two sets of automatic doors. There were planters full of the things, pumping out their bulbous effusions into the small, square space. It was as if the riffraff

coming in off the street were being fumigated in a sort of airlock before being passed into the main reception area.

I had come to research the heraldry and corporate logo-strategy of the city and was visiting it at home so to speak. I was impressed with the reception area, which felt cool and swish, like the foyer of an upmarket hotel. All I needed to know regarding the pictorial identity of Newport was to be found in glass cases and I spoke quietly into my pocket tape recorder as I read and marvelled.

I am not what is called by educationalists a 'visual' person. I have to interpret what is in front of me through the medium of words and tell myself what my eyes are reporting to my brain. Then, when I hear what I'm saying, I can see what I'm looking at. This is something that those not similarly afflicted seem unable to understand. More and more I find explanations and instructions are given in the form of crude pictures, without verbal annotation. I spend my life in a state of subclinical bewilderment.

A PROPER CHERUB

Whereas by order in council made the twenty-third day of July nineteen ninety-six Her Majesty the Queen has been graciously pleased to order that the armorial bearings of the former Borough Council of Newport may be borne and used by Newport County Borough Council....

The technical description of the Civic Badge is:

Arms: Or, a chevron reversed gules the shield ensigned by a cherub proper. Supporters: on the dexter side a winged sea lion or, and on the sinister side a sea dragon gules, the nether parts of both proper, finned gold. Upon a compartment comprising waves of the sea proper.

What this actually means is: A gold shield with a red V and a cherub (not a cherry) on the top. The cherub is described as proper. I assumed that this was because, being only a head, it had no 'nether parts' and therefore no opportunity to display those promising little wrinkly bits that the Old Masters so often failed to obscure. No, it just means that it is painted in its natural colours, like the tails of the sea monsters that support his perch above the equally proper waves.

Those supporters are a sea lion (gold) and a sea dragon (red).

That's a fairly ordinary lion and a bog-standard dragon, with fishes' tails where their back legs ought to be. The lion is on the dexter, or right-hand side, the dragon on the sinister, or left.

Wait! – I hear you cry. Isn't the dragon on the *right?* Yes, he is. But that is one of the great secrets of Heraldry. When you look at a coat of arms, you must imagine it's being borne on the shield of a warrior or the breastplate of a knight. The right and left sides are those of the bearer of the arms. Not yours. So there.

They face each other forever, the dragon and the lion, so different on the surface, so similar below. They are united in a common purpose – keeping the cherub's head above water.

THE MYSTERIOUS FLYING MONKEY

You see him here, you see him there – the flying monkey's everywhere! The logo used by the City Council appears on vans and bins and buses and all the civic infrastructures throughout Newport.

But what is it? Having always described it to my own satisfaction as a flying monkey and having had that description unquestioningly accepted by the people to whom I mentioned it, it never occurred to me to seek its true identity or provenance.

But when I stepped through the outer doors of the Civic Centre and was seduced and fumigated by the scent of hyacinths trapped in the airlock between the city's pure heart and its grubby body, I felt an inexplicable kinship with the monkey. So I asked the lady at the information desk and she directed me to a glass case where its *fons et origo* was pinpointed with Darwinian exactitude.

It is not a monkey at all, but a beast of an entirely different genus and element. It is a winged sea lion (not a sealion, which is a whole different kettle of fish…) and has been adapted from the main coat of arms.

He was commissioned in 1991 and introduced in August 1992. He is (I quote) "a visual projection of the Council's organisational character, what it stands for and how it is expected to behave. The corporate colours of green and yellow are distinctive and impactful, reflecting quality and professionalism, the green echoing the city's environmental awareness and the yellow, long associated with Newport, providing a bright contrast…"

My monkey had become a lion, but there was now another question – Yellow? Why has yellow been long associated with Newport?

But what I really wanted to see were the famous murals by Hans Feibusch which were commissioned by the Council in 1960. Feibusch began on them in 1961 and they took him four years. The twelve panels show the history of Newport, beginning with the Celtic settlement and ending with (wait for it!) the building of George Street Bridge *(ta-da!)*.

I suppose, though, that Newport was moving forward at that time and that Feibusch had simply brought the story up to date. The Council has already acknowledged the fact that the city is again moving fast and that George Street Bridge is no longer hot news. Plans are afoot to continue the story and more murals have been commissioned but the artist originally chosen to carry these out has since died and at the time of writing there is a search in progress for someone else to take on the commission.

But they'll never find another Feibusch. Hans Feibusch was a German Jew who lived through virtually the entire twentieth century. He was born in Frankfurt in 1898. In 1930 the Prussian Academy of Arts in Berlin awarded him the German Grand State Prize for Painters, but in 1933 and unable to work in Germany, he fled to Britain where he spent the rest of his life. In 1937 in Munich the Nazis held an art exhibition of what they called *Entartete Kunst,* or *Degenerate Art.* Feibusch was represented there, alongside Klee, Kandinksy, Chagall and Picasso. Between 1938 and 1974 he painted forty murals for churches and cathedrals, and even some for Clough Williams Ellis in Portmeirion. During those years he converted to Christianity, but returned to Judaism before he died in 1998.

In accordance with Feibusch's mischievous tradition, some of the faces in the murals were modelled on leading councillors and council officials of the time. A younger artist, Phyllis Bray, assisted Feibusch on the Newport murals by painting all the landscape backdrops. And almost before the paint was dry on the last panel, he and Phyllis packed up their brushes and went on to do his most celebrated work, *The Trinity in Glory,* in the Church of St Alban the Martyr in Holborn.

But now as I wandered around the upper gallery looking at the murals, the day to day business of the Civic was clearly carrying on regardless. I was approached by a brisk young lady who asked if I was "here for the procurement training". I found this interesting, believing that one could still be sent to jail for that. I assured her that I was in no way so inclined and in an attempt to cover my confusion I turned my attention to a notice on the wall.

It seemed the murals were in the process of being refurbished as there was evidence of their deterioration. The methods being employed were described in detail:

> This area of unstable paint has been faced up to prevent loss before phase two of the conservation campaign begins; please do not touch. The material used in facing up is Japanese tissue paper which has very long fibres allowing the tissue to conform to the contours of the surface without breaking. The adhesive is isinglass which is a fine glue made from the swim bladder of the sturgeon infused in water with the addition of a small amount of honey. This is a traditional adhesive with many advantages. It has low surface tension, is water-soluble, is very strong and gels at room temperature.

I enquired later as to the nature of the deterioration. Was it due to the nature of the paint Feibusch used – special *trompe l'oeuil* oil paint which dried to look like pastel and was specially made for him by Winsor and Newton – or to its being done on dodgy plaster? One expert told me it was because the roof leaked, another that there were water tanks in the ceiling above. One mentioned condensation and added that they were in sore need of a clean, anyway. But in the *South Wales Argus* it was reported that the walls were suffering from being compressed by the weight of the clock-tower. I suspected that this might be the last outcry of one of the disaffected nay-sayers who was still fuming after being over-ruled in 1963.

TESTING THE SYSTEM

All calls to Newport Council are made by dialling a single, all-purpose number. I rang it once when I was trying to find details of a place I had come across many years ago during what was my first and only contact with Newport until I moved to South Wales at the end of the eighties.

It was a children's home. Fairly new, very sixties. I had come there to bring two children from Birmingham in the days before Monmouthshire was in Wales. Before I ever dreamed of ending up in this part of the world. Before I had become the grizzled old cynic who set out to write this book about the city to which I came late and ignorant. I wondered if I could ever find the place again so as to lay to rest two little ghosts that have followed me silently for many years.

My husband had newly qualified in social work. He had joined the Child Care Department and was in the early stages of authority, more at ease with the power than the responsibility. He had been told to take two children from Balsall Heath to be placed in a care home in the Newport area, there being no place for them locally. Because they were two little girls, he had to take a female chaperone. Since nobody from the department was available I was deputised.

The children were waiting for us outside their house, along with most of their family. A young woman in a mustard-coloured suit stepped forward and spoke to my husband. The girls were about five and seven, beautifully dressed in immaculate *salwar kameez*, tiny copies of their mother who was sobbing in the arms of an older woman. A soft bag lay on the pavement between them and they stood silent, watching us. Then, as the mustard suit took them by the shoulder and started to steer them towards the car, the mother screamed. A sound I shall never forget. She tore herself from the arms of her comforter and grabbed the girls, still screaming, the shrill noise rising and falling like a siren, on and on.

The girls were prised firmly from her arms and steered towards the car. Mustard suit explained that the mother was going into a sanatorium and the girls were to be taken into care until she returned. She said this had been agreed, but she had been unable to explain our presence to the distraught woman. None of us spoke Urdu. I remembered the leaflet that we had at the Family Planning clinic where I worked as a volunteer. I searched my memory for any phrase that would help. I knelt on the pavement beside the girls and pointed to myself. *Soshal Varkar*, I said, and smiled. It was as if I had introduced myself as the Archdemon.

Their mother was still screaming as we drove off. On the way one of the girls was violently sick. My husband was angry, as if it were my fault. I said nothing, sat smiling and singing quietly to the girls in the back of the car but they just stared with their huge frightened eyes. I held their bony little bodies gently all the way to Newport, wondering how on earth any of the family would manage to come all this way to keep in touch.

The place seemed to be a long way from the centre of the town. My husband fumed. Eventually we drew up in front of a group of long, low cellblocks. We handed the girls over to a woman who asked about them over their heads, then took hold of one of the soft little pierced ears and tutted at the gold hoop. "These will have to go," she said. I was about to plead but I caught my husband's eye and said nothing.

On the way back I questioned the humanity of what had just been done and my husband said that I should not ask questions because I wasn't qualified to make a judgement. Unless I could make any sensible suggestion as to how to get the smell of vomit out of the car, I had better keep quiet. So I didn't tell him the news I had received that morning – that I was pregnant with our first child. I was afraid he would say that that, too, was all my fault.

I decided that I must find the place again, if only to see if it still has the air of the purpose-built stalag that I have carried in my head all these years. To lay to rest the two little ghosts, with their oiled, aromatic plaits and their huge eyes, whose silent acceptance has been an enduring reprimand. All I knew was that it had once been in the bailiwick of the Newport authorities and that it might be so still. I felt sure that the Social Services Department would be able to tell me. There might be a senior childcare officer who would remember the home, know if it still existed.

I looked in the telephone book for Newport City Council and found a full-page advertisement directing me to that single number. A recording welcomed me to *Newport City Contact Centre* and told me that my call *would be recorded and monitored* and offered me the option of conducting my enquiry in Welsh. It went on to say that, *due to the volume of calls* their response would be *delayed by approximately...thirty seconds...*and then a real voice asked how it could help. "May I speak," I said, "to the Social Services Department". "May I ask," said the voice, "what it is regarding?" "What *what* is regarding?" asked the pedant in me before I could trip it up.

I said that it was most likely the Childcare Department I needed and was asked again "what it was regarding". Was it a referral? Did I have the name of the child? When I asked if I might just speak to someone in the department of my choice I was made to understand that the choice was not mine to make. I started to tell her what I wanted to know and she kept interrupting: "What is the name of the place", "Where is it?", "I need to know that before I can decide who to put you through to". The questions felt intrusive, like being quizzed before a full surgery of prurient listeners as to "What exactly is the problem?" by an overzealous receptionist standing like a night-club bouncer between the whole wide world and 'Doctor'.

Twice I was told she would put me through somewhere and got long, almost unbearable swathes of soul-destroying music, a ghastly loop tape of Sinatra, while she attempted to do it. Twice she came back to tell me that this was not the right department. Clearly she was paraphrasing a half-understood question out of earshot on my behalf and I wanted to put it myself. "Childcare" I said firmly. "Put me through to Childcare." I was told that they had access only to the duty team and that they were all far too young to remember the sixties but... and the music started again. I waited. And waited. Maybe I was too dull to know what I wanted but it sure as hell wasn't Ol' Blue Eyes. So I hung up.

I dialled again. Another operator started asking the same questions and insisted that she had to ask them in order to help me. I told her I'd been through it all before and that all I wanted was a wee wordette with someone in the childcare department. She honestly tried, but they were all "in a meeting" for the next three-quarters of an hour. She told me, though, that when I rang again I should ask straight away for the duty childcare team. So an hour later, I did.

"What is it regarding?" asked yet another voice. "Geographical location of temporary provision units" I replied, with as much authority as I could muster. And I was put through straight away. A young lady called Eleri answered. I asked my question, told her the circumstances and she said that, although she couldn't answer me herself since this would have been before her time, she would ask somebody else and get back to me.

She rang within five minutes. She had spoken to her supervisor (the senior childcare officer I had been hoping to find all along) and she thought it might have been a home that is no longer open. She told me the name of it. "Coed Glas..." I wrote. "As in 'green wood'?" I asked, surprising myself.

I found the place out near Abergavenny; it's used for other purposes now. It still looks a bit like a POW camp, though the grounds are beautifully designed and well-tended. On the day I found it there was an entirely fortuitous thunderstorm. I stood under dripping trees looking at it for a while, remembering. Then I turned on my heel and walked away.

CENTRAL

THE BUS STATION

At the inner end of Kingsway it lies, concrete and uninviting. Much like the one in Cardiff, but in Cardiff the buses slink up alongside the bays, while here they nose in at an angle, like half a Christmas tree. Each one knows its own place and slots itself into it like a piglet to a teat. Then it sucks up its passengers and creeps out backwards with a merry beeping sound, glad to get away from the long crepuscular tunnel floored with lumps and puddles that are best left uninvestigated.

For a long time the bus station was the only major building in that area that actually faced the river, although a row of buildings with their backs to it on the other side of a whizzing dual carriageway made sure that you couldn't actually see it. Now, though, the rear view of the Riverfront Centre hints that there might be something worth looking at over there, though an amazingly complicated press-a-titty/run-for-it pedestrian crossing makes sure only the highly-motivated go over there to find out.

One thing, though, that the bus station can justifiably boast of, is one of the finest ladies toilets in the city. It has a wonderful curved tiled entrance with a huge mosaic of an unmistakable lady and the gender designation – *Merched* – clear as daylight. How very different from the posh red brick ones on Gilligan's Island, where the logos are so stylised and the innards so minimalist that you can easily meet up with a member of the opposite sex in a compromising position and never know for sure which of you is in the wrong.

The downside is that this excellent amenity shuts at five thirty on the dot and so does the underground one with the wrought-iron

railings in Austin Friars. I know this, having made the dash. This means that a person facing an hour-plus journey on the six thirty to Brynmawr must use the unisex, self-cleaning, French-inspired doings at the other end of the bus station. This opens grudgingly on the insertion of twenty pee and closes with an ominous clang. Females – remember to back in and don't whatever you do, look down. 'Nuff said.

However, I have found that, if taken short after half past five, it is better to avail oneself of the Ladies in Ferris's Café, though this costs a little more because one has to buy chips so as not to feel beholden. *Faiblesse oblige*, as it were.

The beggars in the bus station are fly and feathered. They lurk in twos and threes, all with an eye for the main chance. They are disabled, dirty and hard as nails. They have clearly instructed one of their number to make the first approach to the punters. He is a pale unprepossessing pink and he has a foot missing. His left leg ends in an ugly little knob. He hobbles forward and as his presence registers the bits of crisp and crumb start to fall like manna. On an unseen signal, the heavy mob move in and take over. In seconds they have been and gone, cleared up and scarpered. The lone, limping beggar moves in again.

They are a breed apart, the Newport pigeons. They patrol the bus bays like socially motivated rats, clearing up after the departed passengers, prising squashed chips off the pavement; straight swaps for squirts of shit. For now they have the territory to themselves.

Once there were human horrors lurking in the shadows but recently a change has taken place. I came here late one night and observed it for myself. At first I couldn't quite understand what had happened and it took me a while to work it out. The effect is amazing! With a single stroke some clever soul has blown a frost over the domain of the hoodies, the gangstas, the malevolent chavs, the whole boiling of disaffected youths who have hitherto looked upon the shit-blitzed bus station as their own domain. The management are now playing music for them. Quite loud.

Not the repetitive, soul-sucking *thugga-bugga-bugga* that blares from their cruising cars, but the slippery sweet easy-peasy-cheesy-listening stuff that wallpapers tearooms and the roosting places of the refined elderly. And now, though they are still at liberty to form their menacing platoons, they can do nothing. They cannot rumble to *Charmaine*. They cannot march to *Nimrod*. So they no longer foregather in their usual numbers. I miss them. Like a plague of ants after it's over, I wonder uneasily where they are now – but I don't want them back.

Music hath charms, indeed, to soothe the savage breast. But sometimes, in the evening, when the shops close and the dispirited queues, burdened with bags, shuffle resignedly up to the grubby buses, showing their passes and climbing awkwardly aboard, I do wish they wouldn't play the theme from *Schindler's List*...

NEWPORT MUSIC

However, the bus station is not the only place where you can hear music. Arrive betimes on a weekday morning and you'll hear it everywhere. The whole city is alive with it. Listen. Hear the swelling ground bass of the traffic where it's moving freely, the syncopated stutter where it isn't. Be aware of the half-songs of the mobile phones, not issuing forth from the little instruments clapped to the undersides of the awkwardly tilted heads but from the moving mouths that come and go in a complicated dance on the daily stage. Hear the many levels of excited recitative that threaten at any moment to blossom into full-scale aria.

Walk along the underpass towards the castle and hear how each isolated thread of conversation is woven into an atonal symphony amplified by the lavatorial tiling into something a little threatening. Here are uncomfortable echoes of twentieth-century experiment; there is no immediately discernible melody and the sounds make sense only to the individual instrumentalists who are collaborating on the score as they go along.

Come out again into the open air and they unravel into individual lines of operatic dialogue – *Bella figlia dell'amo-o-re* – as the older man, now away from home, converses with his invisible mistress and the smartly-dressed young woman commiserates with her absent friend – *iniquo traditor!* – oh, it all goes on.

W. S. Gilbert missed a treat. He'd have love-hated this:

Monday Morning Mobile Rap

Each momentary fragment
Is a subspecific segment;
Little bits of him and her that all add up to us:
You're kidding me! Never!
Speakcha soon. Whatever.
You'll have to give it welly, mate, because I'm on the bus.
Each manifestation
Has its own interpretation
Anything from patter-song to hip-hop rap;
From the language of the street
To the openly effete:
Didja Geddit? Narmean? Loadafuckincrap!
Oh, Hello, it's Felicity
I think you left a text for me –
I didn't quite catch that, so could you say again?
Little bits and pieces
Of examples of our species;
Can you hear me mother? Is that you? I'm on the train.
Oh, rant and whinge and cavil
Tell the truth and shame the devil
No-one gives a monkey's even though they're not alone
Lovey-dovey making up
Sorry man, you're breaking up
I haven't time to talk to you because I'm on the phone.

Sometimes, however, the music is specific and identifiable. There is often an elderly green-and-yellow pixie playing a tin whistle to a backing tape in the tunnel entrance to John Frost Square. Presumably he lurks there for the echoes from the shiny surface of the Chartist mosaic. Now and again a coin will drop into his hopeful hat. Every so often he will stop blowing and let the recording take over while he takes a whiff and chats to passers-by. I have seen this for myself in broad daylight with not a drop taken.

There's music to be had for up-front money, too. The after-dark scene in Newport is not a thing I've explored personally but a number of young musicians I know and love have tested their sticky wings at TJs, probably the best known of Newport's clubs. It prides itself on its atmosphere of mucky tat and it claims to be the place where Kurt Cobain proposed to Courtney Love, though what it was that he proposed I am not in a position to say.

There are seemlier lunchtime concerts in the Riverfront on the first Wednesday in every month, recently a flute and guitar duo, soon a mezzo-soprano with a pianist, and in the Newport Centre there are more youth-oriented offerings. Groups like *Delirious?* – apparently a devoutly Christian outfit from Littlehampton in Sussex, and soon *The Zutons*, a Liverpool band with, I am told, "a glam-rock-boogie vibe and now with more soul than previously demonstrated on their debut record". Perhaps in the interim they have been listening to *Delirious?*

Littlehampton? Liverpool? Does Newport have no native sounds? Indeed it does. I have already mentioned Goldie Lookin Chain, the *jeunesse dorée*, the streetvoice of the city. Their first album was even called *Straight Outta Newport*, but only in America. Here, presumably because of the unsaleability of the city, that title was deemed counter-productive. So, with a sort of ghastly irony typical of the group, it was called *Greatest Hits*. They are a disparate lot, the Chain, with their gratuitous sportswear and their Southwalian street-cred. They have disclaimed their given names in favour of a series of jolly sobriquets. There's Eggsy (AKA The Fresh Prince of Cwmbran) and Maggot, Dwain Xain Zedong and Adam Hussain and others too numerous to mention, since any three may turn out to be one of the others, if you get my drift. They've now made two albums of cringeworthy rip-off rap that for some reason makes me smile. Not a superior smirk, either. A smile of pure affection. I heard sounds like these ages ago when my own boys were starting to make music. The experimental noises, the giggling, the collaborative lyrics, the throwaway, there-for-the-rhyme daftnesses that are delivered as though they were profundities. The occasional little witticism taken to excruciating limits and then left to collapse in a puddle because nobody knows quite what to do with it. But who is kidding whom? If their success continues their material may soon be deconstructed by academics and put on the GCSE syllabus, but for now I take it for what it is. A joke. And all the more acceptable for being a knowing joke. They send up our greedy, litigious society and while we laugh and tap our knowing noses, they send up the music, too, with all the straight-faced double standards of the tabloid press. The lads are buffoons but they're nobody's fools.

And it's all made out of Newport. The language of their lyrics is a half-heard, half-handknitted patois. It bonds and excludes. It mentions streets, clubs and cafés, nudging Newport citizens with a conspiratorial wink and making no concession whatsoever to a wider audience. Now, that's clever. Make 'em look, make 'em find out. And, with a bit of luck, they will. It worked for Liverpool.

I know that perhaps after all the whole enterprise is utterly cynical and they have seen the unlovelier aspects of The 'Port as a sort of sad novelty and its drifting citizens as a niche market. But does that matter? Someone has to sing the city. It's a job waiting to be done, however and by whoever. Whatever.

THE SOUTH WALES ARGUST

In March 1989 I started work in the newsroom of the *South Wales Argust*. No – this is not a typo. That terminal "t" is part of the title when spoken by the majority of those in its circulation area. It is the *Argust* when its content is discussed in the pub. More properly the "nightly *Argust*", for although it has a lunchtime edition, it is essentially an evening paper. Part of going home, of teatime and *what's on the telly?* When the management board decided to buy a racehorse in the early nineties, they called it Knightly Argus. The "K" was their little joke. But they ignored the "t".

Perhaps they couldn't hear it. It is just a little flick of the tongue against the back of the teeth, a terminal lick to finish off the sibilant, slightly apologetic and occasionally almost imperceptible. But it *is* there, bless it.

It is rather like the definite article reduction in the North of England, where 'the' is nipped into a furtive gesture which pays grudging respect to the particular when passing on a piece of information. Before a consonant it is as though the tongue were cleaving to the roof of the mouth in an awkward hesitation, but before a vowel or a swallowed aspirate you can hear it clearly. Thus the Bradford evening paper is *t'Argus*, while that of the southeasterly coming-together of the Valleys is *the Argust*.

This piece of happy vernacular delighted me, bridging the gap between the land I left behind and that in which I had arrived.

JOINING THE ARGUS

The editor of the *Yorkshire Evening Post* gave me a reference; the editor of the *South Wales Argus* welcomed me cautiously. I was assigned to the Supplements Department under a dapper little chap called Rodney Smith. Rodders was a star, a wit, a man of words. Despite the oppressive heat in the low-ceilinged office, he wore a three-piece suit with the waistcoat fully buttoned. He had installed a huge swiss-cheese plant on top of the filing cabinet behind his head and he peered from its fronds like a well-groomed marmoset. I liked him instantly, not least because he had heard of me and declared himself pleased to be working with "someone who can really write". He introduced me to his second-in-command, Bob Rogers who, in shirtsleeves and sandals, shook my hand and asked gruffly "what do you want a job for? – you'll soon be dead". Poor chap, he had been fantasising about a female assistant for some time and I duly apologised for failing to live up to his expectations of innocence and pulchritude. He forgave me and we became – and still are – friends.

Not long after that, Rodders was summarily dismissed, apparently for moonlighting on the *Daily Sport*, though why that should have been a sacking offence I did not understand. He asked me to take care of his houseplant, which I faithfully did. For the next two years, 'Supplements' consisted of Bob and me and the magnificent *Monstera Deliciosa*, which was always known as Green Rodney and, for all I know, still is.

We wrote advertising features. Sometimes two or three per issue. The whole idea of these advertising features was that they should be 'editorially led' – written, that is, as pieces of investigative journalism, apparently without regard to the feelings of the businesses concerned. Those businesses, however, would take out advertising space on the page where the piece appeared. So if waiters had dirt under their fingernails, if you actually saw rats in the premises or dodgy goods being offered for sale, it was tacitly understood this was not to be included in the copy. I was called to the Editor's office twice in as many days. Once because I had said something negative in a piece, which wouldn't do, and once because I had allowed a punter to see what I had written and changed something in accordance with their wishes, which was just as bad. It was a fine line I had to walk. I was employed to write such things as would be pleasing to the subject but it had to have the appearance of serendipity. This was because the paper's remit only allowed for a certain proportion of advertising matter, so these specialised pieces had to pretend convincingly that they were no such thing. But they were.

BEING ON THE *ARGUS*

The best bit of being on the *Argus* was the other people who worked there. The paper, like All Gaul, was divided into three parts: News, Sport and Features. I was part of Features, along with Bob, Annabel who wrote girlie pieces, Peter who wrote news-based pieces and the marvellous Mike Buckingham who could turn his hand to anything and is, at the time of writing, still there, fearless and opinionated as ever.

From the first I was not wholly at ease in the newsroom but did my best to settle in. The Features Editor, a lady of estuarine speech and extraction, clearly found me uncongenial. There was a series running called 'A Day in the Life...' and a journalist would be chosen to follow the daily routine of some pillar of the community (or horny-handed son of toil) for the whole of their working day. It was with an ill-concealed snigger that she despatched me to report on 'A Day in the Life of a Sewage Worker' and it turned out to be one of the most enjoyable days I ever had.

I met up with my team at a depot in Risca. We then went up to the top of the Western Valley, into the playground of Nantyglo Comprehensive, where the first chamber was to be found, and thence followed the sewerage down, checking for blockages, bursts and seepages as far as Aberbeeg.

I went down manholes, waded in distillations of waste and saw for myself the thousand and one different configurations of damp tissue paper. When we knocked off for the day, the chaps told me that the effluent would carry on without us all the way to Newport, where it would be collected in huge holding tanks at St Brides, out past the lighthouse, and released twice a day into the outgoing tide.

I wrote the prose piece that evening; the following poem came later, proving that genuine experience, however come by, is never wasted.

Miaow, There Goes Mr. Brown

Dedicated to the critic who pooh-poohed a poet's description of an old tom cat "slinking like sewage", saying that the simile added nothing to the picture, on the grounds that "sewage does not slink".

People who tinker similes for a living
Test them like pots; they listen carefully
To see whether they strike the proper note

And then they turn them up the other way
To see if they hold water.
Once, underground, researching for a piece
On others' occupations, I walked tall
And carefully along a narrow channel
That carried waste from somewhere to the sea.
I learned the lingo. Rags are dirty debris
That clogs the sides of pipes; the real curse
Of menstruation. Spiral cascades take
Things – out of body out of mind – whizzing
Through flumes and bouncing down stone steps, speeding
The maceration of lumps. My companions,
Who loved and understood their plashy world,
Guided me gently through the truth of it.
One of them drew me suddenly aside
With "Whoops, my flower! Here comes Mr.Brown!"
A corky orange turd bobbed in the stream.
Reaching the aggregation of wellingtons
Interrupting the flow, it changed direction;
Transformed into a ginger fugitive,
An old tom cat avoiding confrontation,
It slunk past in the shadow of the wall.

Other assignments followed. I was asked to take on the job of Farming Editor, having had a hand-to-mouth smallholding in Yorkshire. This, however, did not last long. My own tiny farm had been a way of life rather than a business and I was totally innocent of the political and financial workings of the agricultural industry. I took up listening to *The Archers* and raiding the farming pages of the *Western Mail* but it was only a matter of time before I was sussed. The farmers of Wentloog found me irritatingly underinformed and said so. The farming page was pulled altogether.

I was also, for a while, allowed to write a fortnightly column 'Afterthoughts', which alternated with a political gossip-column by Paul Flynn, who was our Member of Parliament. He still is, and has been extremely helpful in the writing of this book. He remembers our small liaison with pleasure, though we slipped past one another like ships in the night, settling turn about into the other's still-warm spot. But the Features Editor said she "couldn't see the point of it" and it was stopped.

The Arts Council offered to subsidise a small, regular column which would highlight what was going on in Literary Gwent and showcase occasional local talent. It became a nightmare. When news was thin on the ground the Editor would shout for more and more of 'The Write Stuff' and I would type up in-tray submissions of variable quality against the clock.

I felt like the Sorcerer's apprentice, making more and more copy, craftily upping the font size, double-spacing the poems, anything to fill the demand for words. I lost sleep over that assignment. This was where Newport first read the poetry of Keyvan Ghaemmaghami, the Iranian bus driver whose honest, relentlessly cheerful verses have been mentioned in dispatches from as far away as Cardiff – in Peter Finch's *Real Cardiff Two*, no less – when Keyvan, at the wheel of his double-decker, once ferried Peter between his territory and mine

I did TV criticism, taking turns with the other Features staff. We did a week at a time for an extra fifty quid. We watched the prime-time regulars and the ongoing sagas and we agreed among ourselves to champion one soap each. Mine was *EastEnders*. I once overheard two ladies discussing my appraisal of an episode of *Coronation Street* with which they were clearly at odds. One consoled the other "Never mind, it's Peter's turn next week and he'll put her straight". We had begun to attract factions! I was delighted. I was even appointed second-string music critic for a while, but soon these extras, too, were axed.

The important word at the *Argus* was 'Gwent'. Newport had recently found itself in the newly-created county and the *Argus* was suddenly the standard bearer for this new authority. There was an ongoing insistence on the word's being used as often as possible. We were told to seek the Gwent connection in all breaking news. Woe betide anyone who ignored this prime directive. I was severely censored when I wrote a piece on the 1990 Monmouth Show and tried to express the feelings I was left with. "This was Monmouthshire" I wrote. "Here, just for today, Gwent did not exist." "The *Argus*" I was told, "is all about *Gwent*".

I never quite put my finger on what that meant, but as the paper gradually disengaged itself from what it soon presented as elitist interests and dissolved before my eyes from a broadsheet to a tabloid, I was reprimanded for choosing to interview Julian Mitchell rather than Jeff Banks. And for using "a word that nobody has heard of" (it was *indigenous*).

I interviewed Anthony Hopkins on a lovely summer day when he was anxious to take his mother out to the Gower. I cut the interview time to a minimum and he thanked me. It was just after he'd finished making *The Silence of the Lambs* and he demonstrated to me the disgusting lip-smacking of Hannibal Lecter. I had read the book and we talked about it, laughing occasionally like pair of fools. I concluded the piece with my suspicion that Hannibal might bring him an Oscar, which it later did. But, oh, it seems I had been expected to "get him talking about his hell-raising days because that's what our readers want to know about". And I couldn't escape the feeling that the orchestrated change to Gwent had something to do with the shift in perception. Silly of me.

LEAVING THE *ARGUS*

They sacked poor Bob. I came to work one Monday morning and found that the layout of the office had changed. Someone else was sitting at my computer terminal, which had been re-allocated to the sportsdesk. I went to see the Editor and he said that there was now no specific place for me in the newsroom and I would have to fadge as best I could. I said that as I was demonstrably redundant, I should perhaps be offered some remuneration to go away. He said that redundancy and Redundancy were two different things and it was not incumbent upon the *Argus* to offer recompense. He said that all he could do was waive my notice and if I would go immediately I could have next month's money without working for it. He smiled conspiratorially as though this was a secret favour just between the two of us. So, with as much *chutzpah* as I could summon up, I put everything that was mine into carrier bags, stole several cuttings from Green Rodney and turned my back on the *Argus* forever.

I was too much of a wimp to sue for constructive dismissal. It hurt for a while, but I got over it. The experience has left me with a huge swiss-cheese plant of my very own and an undeniable affection for the grubby town that suddenly became a city.

NOT WAVING BUT DROWNING...

Nobody seems quite sure when the *Steel Wave* arrived to fill the awkward space left between the new ring road and the river. According to thisisgwent.co.uk it was erected in 1990, but newport.gov.uk informs us that it was created in 1991. This is perhaps not as paradoxical as it appears; it would account for the thing's air of being insufficiently conceived.

Its creator, Peter Fink, has made another wave since then – the Mersey Wave. This is a much bigger wave than Newport's and it lights up. It was originally installed in Liverpool in November 2003, but was taken down again early in 2004, after it was discovered that in certain wind conditions it 'moved in a way that was not anticipated'. It was reinstated in 2005 after extensive modifications. Newport's wave is a less ambitious but much more stable structure.

There isn't much to it, really. It depends how you look at it. If you see it from a train coming over the bridge, it looks like an M-for McDonald's, while from the other side of the river it looks like a comatose comma. Make up your own mind. Look at it from anywhere at a distance but don't come too close, because at arm's length it will break your heart.

It was created, says the blurb, to pay tribute to steel and to the sea, Newport's sources of wealth and growth. British Steel built it and the familiar paperclip logo is there on the plinth.

But the docks and the works are effectively closed and British Steel has melted into Corus. The new low City Bridge has effectively prevented access by masted vessels and the only contact with the sea now is the twice-daily copping-out of the river, which goes to look at it and report back on a regular basis. That and the brave bladder wrack that grows in sparse clumps in the mud on this western side, combed daily north and south according to the tide.

The only human endeavour left for it to celebrate is the evidence of intrepid climbing by untalented graffiti artists to see who can leave the highest tag and the marksman‑ship of the bright spark who blinded the row of square glass eyes where the curved box-girders meet in a sort of flat crotch at the top. The annotations are of the usual sort. Representations of unfeasible genitalia and dates when assorted saddos *woz ya*. But on the side nearest the river an anguished man has testified to being betrayed by his girl with his brother and a single, mystical

line, in another hand, tops all the rest. It reads "time of death".

Walk a little way towards the Arts Centre and look back at it. Then you will appreciate what is perhaps its greatest handicap. It is red. But not the same red as the railings along the walkway or the lifebelt lockers in its purlieu. Any fashion adviser would have urged the wardrobe people to go for a tasteful contrast rather than a bad match. I wanted to write a poem for the *Steel Wave* but I couldn't. I didn't know where to put the pity and I couldn't work out what to do with the fear.

RIVERFRONT

When I first came to Newport, the red-brick arts and leisure centre, imaginatively named The Newport Centre, was the only big arts venue in the centre of town. It was also the only leisure centre. It had a state-of-the-art swimming pool with a wave machine and a flume and a fitness suite with a jacuzzi and a gym – and what was described as a multi-purpose sports hall.

It was in this sports hall, with the gym equipment pushed back to the walls that I listened to Haydn's trumpet concerto and found a lot to be desired. I was second-string music critic on the *Argus* at the time and had a preconceived idea of what an orchestral concert should look like, feel like and smell like. In all three I was disappointed to the point of alarm. The smell of chlorine as one entered the building was overpowering, though not quite strong enough to obliterate the whiff of armpit from the seriously underdressed workers-out who

came and went on the stairs like Jacob's seraphim. The concert itself had a sort of flat echo as though it were being performed in a box.

This, I feel sure, was the place the *Monty Python* team discreetly portrayed as the Arthur Ludlow Memorial Baths, Newport, which hosted the celebrated Summarize Proust Competition. This ended, if you recall, with the prize being awarded by default to the girl with the biggest tits. Plenty of contenders there would have been, too, among the seraphim.

In 2002 work began on a new riverfront arts centre and progressed at a fizzing rate, the only hold-up being the unexpected discovery and white-knuckle recovery of a mediaeval ship in the footings (*see: Newport Ship*). In 2004 the centre was imaginatively named Riverfront Arts Centre and opened to the public in October.

And in November, with a great explosion in the national news, the Wales Millennium Centre opened in Cardiff. Which was a bit of a bummer. It was truly impressive, all stone and slate and lit-up statements of Welsh identity. And there was the Riverfront, looking for all the world as though it had been cobbled together out of Formica tabletops commandeered from a giant greasy-spoon, or prefabricated in uPVC from which the protective film had yet to be peeled. For, oh, my dears, it was huge and angular and – Heaven help us! – it was duck-egg blue.

Mind you, I saw it first from the bus station. Not its best side.

Since then it has become the arts venue that Newport lacked, bridging the gap between the Newport Centre and the Dolman (*qv*) and is a promise joyfully fulfilled. See it now from the foot of the *Steel Wave* and you'll see the overhanging gallery like the prow of a futuristic ship. Note the honest see-through glass – none of your nasty mirrors. Go inside and check what's on. Share my pleasure in its uncluttered simplicity. Find an excuse to talk to the enthusiastic, friendly staff. Make a mental note that here is a toilet that is accessible and open long after the one in the bus station is shut. And give silent praise for the fact that, like the *Archform* in the railway station, its unfortunate colour is fading by the day.

There is a statue in the foyer. *Deus ex Machina*. Two dancing figures with the colour and touch of steel, made of flat, shiny, riveted-together layers that look remarkably like mud.

They stand stock-still, yet they whizz. It was made by Newport's favourite sculptor, Sebastien Boyesen, and its construction called for a laser scan of the bodies of two living dancers. It is braver than some of his earlier work for the city, but it still has the same reverence for real living forms which underpin the imaginative extension.

I was sitting in the warm, airy café at the Centre, recalling a perilous, bloodyminded, muddyfooted trek along the opposite bank of the river, which I was now observing retrospectively through the glass. There's going to be a riverside path along there one day, but it's not there yet. Well, there is a path, but it hasn't been transformed by the sparkly wand of the developers. I know this because I dragged my friend Jay with me and we found a way onto the riverbank near the eastern end of the new footbridge. Unfortunately, having blundered along in single file, stopping now and then to admire the footprints of the birds we had disturbed and which were now looking at us resentfully from elsewhere, we discovered that there was no way out alongside the Town Bridge. There was nothing for it but to footslurp back again and squeeze out where we got in. I would normally have been horrified that some insensitive citizen should have dumped a couple of bunkbed mattresses in a heap behind Rodney Parade, but they were perfectly placed for Jay to use as a means of scouring Uskmud from his newish trainers, about which I had been feeling really guilty.

Now I was warm and comfortable. There was a cup of tea on the table in front of me and a piece of cake on a plate, waiting. The cakes at the Riverfront are special not only because they are wicked and delicious, but because they also have bizarre and beautiful names. I pulled the plate towards me. Perhaps indeed the Summarize Proust Competition has found its ideal venue. Next time I shall enter: *Poet relaxes in café. Takes forkful of "chocolate sponge lumpy-bumpy". Gets to thinking...*

THE RIVERFRONT WALKWAY

Out of the glass doors of the Riverfront Centre and off along the signposted Riverfront Walkway on the safe side of the river. I want to know how far it actually goes. Does it cling to the banks of the Usk all the way to Pill? Will it take me, at the very least, as far as the new City Bridge? I actually feel a little *frisson* of impending adventure.

Not lot to see though. However, the river is having one of its better days and looking along it I can see the weird phenomenon that fascinates me every time I catch sight of it. The reflection of George Street Bridge is interrupted by a broad band of non-reflecting water and then starts again this side of it. I wonder, as I always do, why this is, and then set off again towards the bridge itself.

Red-painted metal seats with the names of wharves. Pontypool... Blaenavon... The seats themselves are now all that remains of the old mooring-places, which have long since disappeared. They are puddled with rainwater and are the sort that strike cold even through winter clothing, making them unattractive to the naturally nesh and positive no go areas for anyone sharing their life with Farmer Giles.

And now here's a mosaic map, set into the pavement. Newport's trade links. I stand on Asia and look around me. Bombay... Calcutta... names from yesterday. Heidenheim... Kutaisi... names from now. And Newport, in red, brightest and biggest of them all. There's a bit of Australia sticking up at one side, but most of that is off the map. Bizarrely, Newport City Council's coat of arms is right in the middle of Africa. Clearly the map is not to scale.

The walkway stops suddenly; there is a wire mesh fence across it and chaps in hard hats beavering away in the manner of men who know something that other people don't. One of them gives me a fierce look and points away from the river. I have to pick my way round the site and continue my journey on a parallel track.

But I don't mind. There in the cage formed by the wire mesh lies what looks like a pile of huge white pipes – the legs of the new footbridge that will link the riverside walkway on the west side with the riverside walkway on the east. At the moment, though, the latter is still a gleam in the eyes of Newport Unlimited, the consortium formed to oversee the city's regeneration. They are hoping that the footbridge will be finished in time to coincide with the centenary of the Transporter. A competition has been organised by the *Argus* for a name for it. I shall enter. What about Bifrost?

Still musing about my name for the bridge, I make the necessary diversion, keeping my eye on the next landmark on the Walkway. Castle Bingo, which I have already decided is one of the more attractive modern buildings in this part of the city. Clean ochre brick with a curved glass front, reminiscent of one of the more modern casinos in St Malo. I aim for it, working my way back towards the river.

And I discover, by happy accident one of the sudden secrets of Newport. Round the back of ATS Euromaster, The European Tyre Specialists, there is a gathering of what at first appear to be abandoned vans and caravans. I assume they are there for breaking, dead bodies to be plundered for parts. As I come up to the railings for a look, all small hell breaks loose. Around the periphery of the yard are ranged the strangest collection of guard dogs I have ever seen. Teeny weeny scruffy pariah-dogs of vaguely recognisable sorts, each tied to a kennel, spaced at intervals round this pile of abandoned scrap. Around their homes lie a collection of little dishes. They are obviously tended though tethered.

One of them, a near-as-dammit yorkie, is tied to a plastic crate of the sort designed for carrying lesser pets on show-trips and vet-visits. It appears to be at the mercy of a small, importunate rat. A closer look reveals this to be a tiny puppy, like a sliver of Pears soap. As I photograph its mother, it slithers inside the crate and disappears.

All the fierce little watchdogs quiver with brave apprehension. Their shrill barks rise in hilarious crescendo and their tiny teeth snap out a syncopated rhythm. Nobody comes. But as I round the corner and head back towards the river, I see that there are a few newer trailers and in one a woman is making tea. There are generators hooked up and a huge pile of halfburned rubbish hisses in the drizzle. This is a travellers' site, right here between the road and the river and nobody seems to know or care, apart from the teeny weeny dogs watching with their beady eyes from their own little mobile homes.

It sits incongruously alongside the huge yellow building with the spotless car park whose controlling consortium calls it Castle Leisure. Everyone else, though, calls it Castle Bingo.

I am not a bingo aficionado. The ladies from the sheltered flats in Blaina go down twice a week for what they call 'The 'Ousey' and I always wish them luck, but I have no idea what goes on. Oh, at the level of principle I do; random numbers have always fascinated me, but the idea of embarrassing myself with a solitary cry of 'Pig Hooey' or whatever, makes my blood run cold.

The Bingo Bus

The ladies of Blaina are all going south for the 'Ousey.
Flashing their passes, they accrue on the sideways seats
At the front of the trundling bus as it growls down the valley.

The twitter is constant; a narrow, high range, like bats,
Unmoderated in its content, for who can overhear them
Other than dogs and peculiarly sharp-eared children?

They all chew gum. In their youth it was thought unseemly
So they chew very fast to make up for so much lost time,
Redeploying the involuntary motions of old mouths.

They take on their gum like ballast before boarding.
They work it as they talk, quick-flicking it like the shuttles
Of the flannel weavers in days even they don't remember.

Tongues toss the soft pellets like small boys in blankets;
Teeth, false and furious, catch them and roll them ready
For another somersault as the tongues move in again.

And so it goes – *allez-oop!* – *à bas!* – *encore!*
A non-stop pantomime of death and resurrection
All the way down to the doors of Castle Bingo.

There was a TV ad for Castle Bingo once upon a time. It amused me because there was a musical element, where a row of homely lasses cavorted with pads and pens singing "Castle Bingo, play Castle Bingo" and they gave it a short, northern 'a' – *cassle* – but their diction was so bad that it sounded like *Casa*, as in *Casa Nostra*. I imagined that this *Casa Binga* was a secret society, the flouting of whose conventions would result in acts of reprisal and broken legs.

Then the voice-over announcer came in with a positively home counties *Carsle* and the lack of congruence pleased me hugely; it had suddenly become an academic, Arthurian *Castle Perilous*. Now as I look at this undeniably competent piece of architecture I am wondering how they'd sing the praises of this Newport castle, where the 'a' becomes drawn out long and thin, played as a sustained note on the gristly strings at the back of the nose – *cairsle*.

Almost without realising it, I have joined the Riverfront Walk again. Not for long, though. Just a couple more red metal benches and the whole thing peters out round the back of the bingo hall. I can see the City Bridge, though, by peering through the unshapely legs of George Street Bridge, which is now almost overhead. It will have to do.

The walkway ends in an area of tarmac. Overflow parking for the bingo. A staircase goes up onto the bridge. I turn, though, to the area between its legs. From here you can actually get down to the water. Touch the Usk. Feel the mud. There are security cameras trained on the tarmac but the rubbish-strewn riverbank is, to all intents and purposes, Liberty Hall. This is borne out by the little row of objects on the stone shelf at the bottom of the nearside leg. At first glance this looks like some sort of shrine but the nature of the offerings becomes clear on closer inspection. They are small piles of human excrement, their distance from each other formally determined by the size of the human foot. They stand crisp and undecorated, all evidence of personal cleansing having been swooshed away by the naughty vortices created by the aerodynamic underbelly of the bridge. It is all surprisingly clean and clinical, like a French public squattery but without the holes.

I rise above such observations, up the steps onto George Street Bridge.

LOWER DOCK STREET

Déjà vu...

Up from under George Street Bridge and blinking at the light
Of a sudden sort of shininess that doesn't feel quite right;
The unexpected openness of slightly too much sky
That stimulates a wariness that stops you asking why.
This is the curse of memory, the fact within the fiction.
The child too young to understand who picked up the conviction

That something bad had happened that could never be undone;
The reconfigured skyline and the hazy-looking sun
That gilded dusty vistas of irreparable bits
On the mornings after air raids over London in the Blitz...

It gave me the shivers, so much change waiting to happen, so much taken-for-granted dereliction. This is the scary face of urban reconstruction. I decided to cheer myself up by searching for a highly commended restaurant – The Chandlery. National reputation. *Good Food Guide* and a fistful of stars. And a few heartbreaking local reviews with variations on the theme "this place is too good for Newport". I knew it was in Lower Dock Street so I crossed the road and went in search of it. For some reason I was convinced that it would be at the junction with George Street, in the place once occupied by Restaurant Cymraeg, for which I had had to compose an advertising feature for the *Argus*.

This place was presented to me by its proprietor as a breakthrough in quality cuisine; a really *Welsh* restaurant which was sure to attract the tourists. It had not actually opened when I went to see it. The outside of it was very green with thick paint and hanging baskets and the owner explained to me the ethos of the place with an earnestness that has lived with me ever since. It was time, he said, that Newport had a really *good* restaurant. His staff were being trained to a peak of perfection hitherto unknown in the area. "You know when you go into a restaurant and they crumb down before they bring the coffee?" he asked. I said I thought I did. "Well, here," he said, "The staff will crumb down after every course" and he showed me the little dustpan and brush with which they would do it. He beamed. I blenched.

The idea of having someone fussing round between courses calling obsequious attention to my undisciplined eating habits was one that filled me with anxiety. I was reminded of a reading I once gave to the Harrogate Conservative Ladies

Tea Club. All those attending were served beverage and biscuits beforehand and when one of them had a small accident and asked discreetly for a cloth, the Chairman boomed "Have you been a dirty girl, Catherine?" My heart bled for her and I dared not attempt so much as a digestive, just in case. When I stood up to speak each lady fished out her spectacles (all the better to see you with, my dear!) and the subsequent snapping-shut of all those crocodile handbags put me irresistibly in mind of a firing squad. Nevertheless I made a note of his proposed innovation and included it in my copy without comment.

Alas, the Restaurant Cymraeg was dead and gone and had not been resurrected as The Chandlery. Or if it had, the latter, too, had succumbed to the tide of gustatory indifference that typifies Newport street life. I peered into the windows and there were clearly offices within, but whose they were I was unable to ascertain. I trundled on, hopefully. The landscape of half-demolished and boarded-up buildings grew sadder as I drew nearer to the devastated docks.

A flaking yellow door, half-open, gave access to what had once been the Rest Bite Café. I peered inside to discover that it still was. Two very old gentlemen mumbled bacon butties and looked at me dispassionately through columns of steam that rose from big mugs of tea.

THE CHANDLERY

It was later that I found the Chandlery. Yes, indeed it is at the junction with George Street, but on the city centre side. *Aha!* But why was I looking for it? Because I had a rare chance to invite a chosen chap to lunch and was anxious to try the restaurant considered to be Newport's best. I had read about it in one of the Sundays and I wanted to suss it out to see if it would do.

The man at reception was charming. Even though I had just wandered in off the street with unstructured apparel and a rucksack, he gave me a sample menu and a wine list and didn't look as though he didn't expect to see me again. Later I waved both these documents dismissively before the eyes of the aforementioned Chap to see if they lit up a little. And they did.

I booked a table well in advance, met up with The Chap at the station and got a taxi to the end of Lower Dock Street. I was terrified the place would let me down, my date being something of a *bon viveur* and a bit of a wine buff. I needn't have worried. The décor was simple, the art on the walls local and for sale. The lounge area was untrendily comfortable and the first drink went down a treat.

What had I been afraid of? Hard to say. Aggressive Welshness perhaps. A slide of first-division standards since the flush of good reviews. Would there be side dishes of *half n' half** as a concession to street-cred – an insurance against an after-dark brick through the window?

What I found was an excellent restaurant in an unlikely place. The menu was sufficiently cosmopolitan but still reflected the nation. Welsh beef, lamb, cheeses and one carefully selected wine. But when my companion remarked that his choice of lamb had not been served quite as pink as he would have expected, I hissed that he was not on the saltmarshes of Brittany now and should respect the traditions of the country to which I had brought him.

I was proud of Newport and bathed in the reflected glory of what it could do. I sipped Muscat de Beaume de Venise and looked out of the window – across the busy street to the cluttered car park of George Street Furnishers. For a moment I wished for a 'better' view and then didn't. Change the location and you've lost the point.

* Half 'n' half. An accompaniment to takeaway curries and jumbo sausages that consists of half rice and half chips, thereby alleviating the angst of the lager-laden as to whether they should opt for health or comfort in their choice of evening emetic. It also has overtones of political correctness, which I won't go into.

RAILWAY STATION

Newport has only one railway station. You know when you're coming into it. According to which side of the aisle you're sitting, there's either mud and bridges or mud and Sainsburys.

It's a small station with only three platforms. For the most part, trains heading into Wales stop on Two, trains heading out stop on Three. One is for the overspill. The station slopes dramatically, so the doors of the carriages at the rear ends of the long London trains are high above the level of the platform and terrifyingly far away. I have convinced myself that this is why the first class coaches are at the front, thereby avoiding the necessity for the Quality to undertake the ungainly leap.

ANNOUNCEMENTS

They are bi-lingual. Welsh first. Gradually over the years the sound of it has become familiar. I know the names in Welsh of most of the places I need to get to, and understand that those that do not have Welsh names are articulated with a Cambrian stress that distinguishes them from the English announcement which follows. I know that the oft-repeated, half-heard message that includes a phrase that sounds like 'haemorrhoidal hun' is an indication that the train is late. It amuses me that the Welsh is spoken by a man, the English by a woman. The actual announcements are put together electronically so in theory they could both be done in the same voice, but the need to distinguish is paramount, so someone, at some point, has had to make an executive decision as to the gender of the languages.

The departure boards, though, are androgynous. They simply change from one language to the other with an undetectable switch-flick. Now you see it, now you don't. I am easy with this arrangement but sympathise readily with the agony of strangers. Imagine it. The train is standing like a greyhound in the slips, straining upon the start. The departure board is in Welsh mode. And suddenly the difference between 'o' and 'i' takes on a life-changing significance.

TRAINSPOTTING

One of the things most commented upon by travellers who pass through the station is the inevitable group of shifty-looking individuals who lurk on the far end of Platform Two. The trainspotters. I have spoken to them, but they are cagey and don't give much away. I tried to get a look at the tiny notebook of one of them, but he snapped it shut.

My computer, a damn Yankee in its virtual heart, underlined trainspotting in red. I wondered if it was asking for a hyphen so I asked it what it meant. It told me there was no such word as trainspotting and suggested I replace it with transporting or transposing. It seems they don't do this secret thing stateside. They jump freight trains and ride in boxcars but they don't spot. I wonder why.

Last time I was at the station there were two of them, one quite fat and one rather tall, with a small boy who sat on a seat a little way away and appeared to be minding their backpacks. His legs dangled and swung without touching the ground. The two stood waiting. Waiting and muttering to one another in monosyllables without ever taking their eyes off the tracks. Waiting as though for some Intercity Godot whose arrival would mean everything or nothing, depending on the how or the when of it.

I stepped into their scenario and chipped at their concentration with tentative questions which they did not answer. This was not in the script and they were not equipped to ad lib. I smiled and made as if to leave, then turned suddenly and slipped one in, sneakily. "Do you live near here?" "Not me," said the fat one. "I've come from Plymouth. I can see more stuff here in a morning than I see in a week in Plymouth". Then he fell silent again and looked away. I only wish I could tell you what the stuff was, but I'm afraid I never found out. Something warned me not to push my luck and, with a smile at the small boy, who countered it with a blank stare, I took my own notebook back to the buffet.

ARCHFORM

Outside the station stands the sculpture *Archform* by artist Harvey Hood. British Rail commissioned it in the early eighties, in collaboration with the Welsh Arts Council, to "represent the engineering processes and structures fundamental to the building of Britain's railway system", but Newport Council initially rejected it. Paul Flynn MP claims that he saw it "fall off the back of a lorry" in unseemly hugger-mugger and describes it as "a form of abstract art that is best displayed among consenting artists in private". I would not go as far as that, but I confess that when I first saw it I thought it was an air-conditioning vent. In those days it was painted a bright, ugly blue which I took to be a hamfisted attempt to make a virtue of a necessity. But now that it has faded to the same grey as the rest of the forecourt and is more comfortably ventish, I have grown rather fond of it.

ENTER THE DRAGON

Dragon Taxis, with the distinctive yellow-and-scarlet logo on their doors, was formed in 1986 by two drivers who worked together at one of the town's other taxi companies, who persuaded two colleagues to join their new venture. Premises were set up in the Stow Hill Labour Club but, nearly twenty years and two relocations later, their numbers have swelled more than forty-fold and they are the largest fleet in the county. The business is now located at the station and has secured an exclusive franchise for operating the taxi rank there. The company has gone from strength to strength over the years and the business has expanded. Dragon not only do taxis but also deliver parcels and provide uniformed chauffeur-driven vehicles when required. As the number of driver numbers increased, it became clear that the old system of radio communication by voice was becoming more and more inefficient. So the business invested in a computerised system that now dispatches most of the work via a link to each car. This is great fun on the occasions when I go home by taxi after a late occasion, because I live beyond its purlieu and somewhere around Crosskeys the little screen on the dashboard yelps and dies. This means they have gone beyond the satellite location system and are, technically, at my mercy. However, I am told on good authority that the longest journey so far in the company's history was to France – wait and return!

THE THOUGHT POLICE

One day at the railway station there suddenly appeared barriers, with small men in uniform who shook their heads a lot and tutted. The station had been dragged squealing into the twenty-first century and is now every bit as headbangingly frustrating as Bristol Temple Meads. One now has to feed one's ticket into a tiny slot before even being allowed access to the plaform. This is easier said than done when burdened with luggage and there are several sorts of tickets that won't actually go in.

Thousands of small things are no longer possible. You can't dodge onto Platform One to buy a paper. Only those intending to travel are allowed past the police, so you can't meet anyone off a train any more. There is no such thing as a platform ticket. And it means that yet another of the Newport lavatories that used to be available in an emergency is now lost to me forever.

THE CASTLE

Don't, whatever you do, plan a day trip to Newport Castle. There's not much of it left and what there is will either disappoint you or break your heart. The greed of wheels has almost squeezed it out of existence; most of it is now a traffic island. Its can-strewn, bird-beshitten remains are at worst a hangout for hoodies and at best a short cut to Sainsbury's.

There is access of a sort via a pedestrian walkway and the vaulted ceiling in the central tower is actually beautiful, but on balance it is better seen from a distance. Only the east side survives, sandwiched between the main road and the railway and what's left is best seen from halfway across the adjacent Town Bridge. From there, with a bit of imagination, you can see a shadow of its former grandeur. What a position! Right on the bank of the river with a central tower project-ing over a water-gate. At high tide small boats would have been able to enter the castle through it.

On either side are two octag-onal towers with businesslike buttresses. These mark the north and south ends of the original castle, from which a high wall once ran westwards enclosing a roughly rectangu-lar area which now contains the Old Green roundabout and the railway station. At the foot of this great wall was a deep moat which filled with water at high tide.

OK, so who's the King of

the Castle, then? (And who, by extension, is the Dirty Rascal?)

It was the Normans that built the first one, that much is agreed. One of the Marcher Lords that William the Conqueror set up as guardians of his Welsh Borders with a fairly open brief that encouraged a little bit of conquest on the side. The baron whose men first entered south Gwent was Robert FitzHamon and in 1093 he became the first Norman lord of the Manors of Morganwg (Glamorgan) Brecon and South Gwent including the Ford on the Usk (Newport). His chief base in Wales was Cardiff and he built his main castle there but he did a little one on Stow Hill for when he came to visit his outlying tenants.

FitzHamon's castles, though, were more like sandcastles, as they were of the 'motte-and-bailey' sort, where you made a great pile of earth and built a wooden tower on top. The mound was still there as late as 1848 but then it was subsumed into the rubble excavated from a new railway tunnel that passed directly under it. Two or three people have, in the course of conversation, told me that this amounted to sacrilege because the original eminence had marked the actual resting place of the blessed Saint Woolos and it seems rude to contradict. (Anyway, it was in Friar's Road and there are houses on it now.)

There were houses round it then, too – the hovels of the Anglo-Welsh villagers of the Ford on the Usk, who suddenly found they were serfs, bound to the land which now belonged to FitzHamon. They were forced to work two or three days a week on the lord's land for no payment and they could not give their daughters in marriage without his consent. Presumably he also had the right to road-test them first under the Norman tradition of *droit de seigneur.*

Robert FitzHamon, the mighty Lord of Gloucester, Glamorgan and Gwent, left only one child – a daughter called Mabel. She married Robert FitzHenry who was an illegitimate son of Henry I. He succeeded to the Welsh estates in 1107 when FitzHamon died on the battlefield. He didn't bother much with Newport but built a stone castle at Cardiff instead, so he could take good care of a prisoner his father sent to him – his uncle Robert Curthose (which means 'short-arse').

But the story of Newport Castle is a bit of a damp squib. I have distilled all the accounts to this: in 1126 the castle near the river was built from stone quarried from Stow Hill and the Roman barracks. It was built to guard the ford and protect Caerleon and Newport from gangs of marauding Welsh. The first castle was Norman and its

successor was destroyed by the
Welsh. The ruins that still
stand on the bank of the River
Usk remain mainly from
fourteenth and fifteenth
century rebuilding of the third,
thirteenth century castle,
much of which dates from
around 1405 when the castle
was extended and strength-
ened following the sacking of
the area by Owain Glyndwr.
So far as I have been able to
discover he was the only visitor

of any note apart from Jasper Tudor, Henry VII's uncle and guardian
who was supposed to have lived there for a little while at the beginning of the sixteenth century. It never played any significant part in
national politics, and its main function was the day-to-day adminis-
tration of the lordship of Wentloog. Ho-hum.

Mind you, it did have a little burst of usefulness when it was
converted into a brewery in 1810 and continued to serve this useful
purpose until the 1920s when the Ministry of Works took over what
was left of it and swore to preserve the ruins for posterity.

But amazingly even when the remains of the brewery were cleared
out, there was no attempt at archaeological investigation of the site,
thereby perpetuating the long tradition of utter disregard for the
oldest landmark in the city.

CLARENCE HOUSE AND THE NEWPORT
TECHNICAL INSTITUTE

Over the town bridge, then, carefully counting the coats-of-armses
on the pillars *(gold shield with an upside down V and a proper cherub on
the top? Well done! – just testing...)* But the cherubs on the bridge are
never quite proper. It is a Newport tradition that these long-suffer-
ing little faces are fair game for the ad hoc graffiti artist and itinerant
wit. I have seen them heavily made-up, like under-age streetwalkers
plying for trade, pouting beneath layers of Kissing Pink and
Periwinkle Blue. Once real greasepaint had turned one of them into
a Pierrot, with a single tear glittering on its hamster-pouch cheek.

But most often they are forced, like captive beagles, to smoke endlessly, staring up and down-river. Small roosting mudlarks with secondhand ciggies drooping from their expressionless faces. Any Newport exile, walking in dreams across the Town Bridge, will call up the image of a grubby baby with a fag in its gob.

It was under one of those very cherubs that Kurt Cobain and Courtney Love were involved in a minor car crash in December 1991, arguably the most exciting thing the poor little souls had witnessed since the 5th of March 1913, when Harry Houdini jumped off the bridge with his hands manacled and his feet shackled. He was done by the police the week after for obstructing a public highway and for holding a public entertainment on the bridge in contravention of a local bye-law. Mind you, had they thrown the book at him it wouldn't have worried Houdini, who had already demonstrated his skills by breaking out of a locked police cell in Newport Town Hall in 1905.

And at the end of the bridge, at the start of Clarence Place, are two of the saddest buildings in Newport. Here Clarence House faces the Newport Technical Institute across a steady stream of traffic. Both are disintegrating monuments to hopelessness and to stand in front of either of them and look across at the other is a profoundly depressing experience.

The Institute, built on land purchased from Lord Tredegar in 1899, was opened in 1910 to educate the engineers necessary for Newport's future. Its exquisite proportions, pillared portico and distinctive dome are falling daily into disrepair. According to hoardings above the door it has been sold and will 'soon' be reborn as desirable riverside apartments, much as the warehouses and depositories of Butetown have

been gentrified into Cardiff's Bayside scenario. But oh, please – hurry up! The new footbridge is finished and the proposed riverside walk is but a blink away, but bits are dropping off the 'Stute at a rate of nautical miles and the opportunist buddleia is flourishing in its guttering under the torn flag that ripples bravely above the dull green dome. Soon it will celebrate its centenary. If it lives.

Clarence House, on the other hand, opened in 1973, is in its early thirties and could do with a well-placed bomb. That was probably presumed to be my purpose when I was seen on its CCTV, scruffy and be-rucksacked, trying to photograph the front door. I was fidgetting about so as not to catch my own reflection when a uniformed lady, walkie-talkie in hand, issued forth and demanded to know

my purpose. I pointed to the double doors, the left-hand one of which had had its bronze handle wrenched off by vandals. 'Pull', said the engraved legend. 'Please use right-hand door', said the notice above the missing handle. I thought this was funny but she couldn't see the joke. This building houses Newport's County Court and to get in you have to squeeze through half a door, which is situated between a downmarket superstore and an Italian restaurant with unchanging menu whose Mâitre D can't spell. Bless.

From the dilapidated steps of the Institute, Clarence House is a cubic rebuke. When it was new it was a little ahead of its time, faced with blocks of colour like Erno Rubik's Hungarian puzzle which wasn't invented till a year later. Now, though, its two pigments – fake tan and bruise blue – are peeling off like steamed wallpaper. Its flat roof bristles with mobile phone base stations and its unsavoury backside is the last thing you see from the train before coming over the river and entering the station. It, too, was built in hope, to provide office space for all the new commerce that was going to happen and didn't. It is now no more than a half-empty, battered box that could do with being thrown away. I fear it is beyond re-cycling.

SEÑOR COCONUT

Once upon a time there was a Mexican Café in Newport. It was in Griffin Street, and was kept by the Ferris family, who have fed Newport with the sort of food its heart desires for as long as most people can remember.

Charles Ferris, source of so much information in this book, champion of the campaign to save the Newport Ship, the man who keeps and cherishes the bus station chippie, is the son of the proprietors of that café. I asked him what had prompted such a brave break with Newport tradition; surely this was the first whiff of Tex-Mex cuisine ever to waft across the city? Not at all, he replied. It was called the Mexican Café because there was an enormous sombrero hanging on the wall. End of story.

When I was taken Señor Coconut in Clarence Place, I was told that it was a Mexican restaurant, but my suspicions were aroused by the huge inflatable cactus on the counter. Was this, like the sombrero, a minimalist theme statement? A little local in-joke? Was it, I wondered, just another Southwalian eatery after all?

Well, yes and no. The outside was then painted in the special sort of eggy yellow that gets discounted in Focus. I peered in through the window and it looked dark. My companion, conscious that it was now well past his feeding time, forged his way inside. I followed him into the spice-laden gloom.

A charming waitress came to ask if it was our first time. She said the arrangements at lunchtime were different. This was rather like arriving in a strange town to be greeted with a 'Changed Traffic Layout Ahead'sign. Changed from what? Technically this should be of no concern to the newcomer, but it always provokes a *frisson* of unease. Surely the innocent is doubly at risk from both the new layout, which will mean nothing to him, and the old layout which he never knew or understood. What was it at Señor Coconut that was different and from what?

I'm afraid I can't tell you because I have never been back, since I am not fond of Tex-Mex food. But I can tell you that at lunchtime there is a sort of buffet – the waitress brings a large plate and sets the customers loose to collect salad and rice and things from bowls; things that are floating in juices that are red and hot and lumpy. They reminded me of the sort of things you can buy in trays in supermarkets which stick to the underside of the clingfilm as though they had been trying to get out when you weren't looking. I eschewed one that looked as though it had bits of sweetcorn in it and braved another in which all the lumps were brown. It was all right. And the orange juice was really nice.

RODNEY PARADE – HERE BE EVEN MORE DRAGONS

I knew, at the level of general knowledge, that Rodney Parade was the home ground of Newport RFC and when now and again the name 'Newport Gwent Dragons' impinged upon my consciousness I assumed that it was simply a new name for the old club. I couldn't have been more wrong and when I let this misapprehension show in public, like a third nipple or a rude tattoo, I was pointed and jeered at, so that I backed away, blubbing.

So I secretly looked up the history of the Dragons and found out the truth of the matter. The club was established in the summer of 2003 following the WRU's decision to reduce nine professional clubs into five regions. In the summer of 2004 this dropped to four following the unfortunate demise of the Celtic Warriors. *(Oh – did they go to Tir Nan Og, I wondered? Do they play Rugby in the hollow hills with the Little People? – alas, I digress. It is hard for me to concentrate on sport for long.)* This four-club format was apparently an attempt to mirror the successful arrangements in Ireland, South Africa, Australia and New Zealand.

Newport Gwent Dragons officially represent southeast Wales, and play all of their matches at Rodney Parade, often, apparently ousting Newport RFC who have to go and play in someone else's garden. Largely drawn from the Newport RFC and Ebbw Vale RFC, the Dragons were considered one of the weaker regions in the Welsh game, although their coach Mike Ruddock was considered one of the best. So much so that he was headhunted to coach the

national side, and thereby hangs another tale.

They were unfairly perceived at the start of the inaugural season as a side of rejects, a side no one really expected great things of *(Ouch! Sorry; not my grammar!)* However, with strong coaching, a strong work ethic and fantastic team spirit, The Dragons proved their critics wrong. And now comes the *Oh, No* bit.

The naming of the region has caused considerable turbulence because, unlike the stand-alone regions of the Cardiff Blues and Llanelli Scarlets, the Newport Gwent Dragons were a new regional creation who are meant to represent a 'Gwent region'. Some in the Welsh rugby world believed that including the name Newport would alienate some fans in the surrounding valleys including fans of the historic Ebbw Vale RFC. Several names were suggested but all were rejected. In the end, the WRU decided the name for them: the Gwent Dragons. This only lasted a season, because Ebbw Vale RFC went close to bankruptcy, and were forced to sell their stake in the Gwent Dragons to Newport RFC. After this, the name Newport was added to the front of the title. In reality, the side has lost more supporters by including the name 'Gwent' in its title. The crowds supporting the Newport Gwent Dragons average about four thousand – half the number that supported the Newport team that it succeeded. *(Wait – isn't that Newport RFC and don't they still exist? – no – please don't tell me; I really don't want to know.)*

Although controversy surrounding the naming of the region might seem petty, rugby in south Wales is deeply divided amongst hundreds of historic rugby clubs with bitter rivalries. I thought for one precious moment that the new side would have united these splintered factions in some blessed act of union.

Alas, not so. In the weblog of a ruggerlover I found the following, which inspired in me an almost uncontrollable urge to drink bleach. *Obviously as a Newport fan I would have preferred Newport to have remained as the name but that is water under the bridge now and I think we have to stick with the NGD name. Before the regional set up Newport were getting between six - eight thousand*

average crowds, so from an economic viewpoint of the Dragons are ever to be a success, it makes sense to try and encourage the Newport fans (as well as fans from the rest of Gwent) to matches. I just feel that the current marketing is alienating everybody, both in Newport and in Gwent. No-one knows what to shout…

Don't know what to shout, eh? How about *"Dragons!"* or, failing that, *"Get a Life!"?*

THE USK FOOTBRIDGE

As it grew, I liked it. I liked the thought of it, the picture of the brave boulevardiers sauntering over the Usk, making paper boats from their chipwrappers and lobbing them carelessly into the turgid water. I liked the idea of the student quarter, planned round the re-sited University buildings and the green thinking that suggested its denizens should walk or cycle to and fro across the river.

It will be nice, I thought, when they get rid of the last two cranes. In this, though, I was deceived, for the last two 'cranes' proved to be part of the bridge itself. It is a suspension bridge, albeit suspended entirely from the West bank, giving the appearance of a drawbridge that can be whipped up if the students ever become unsettled. But the two great double supports, one leaning out over the river, one leaning back to balance its weight, gave me a bit of a surprise the first time I tried to come to terms with their being a permanent part of the structure. They put me irresistibly in mind of my first sight of synchronised swimming. Perhaps I am the only one who finds this brazen display distasteful. Probably so, since it has recently become an Olympic sport.

Good Lord! I thought. Those white struts are the big bare legs of a swimmer practising her moves. Up she rises from the surface, feet first, twinkling her toes girlishly for a moment then letting her legs flop apart in a slow gesture of artless obscenity that mocks the enforced modesty of mermaids. She holds the pose for a while before doing a series of embarrassing variations on it for as long as she can hold her breath. Then one last waggle of her muscly limbs and down she goes, to re-appear rubberhatted, the right way up, not drowning but waving. The bridge, though, seemed stuck in fuck-me mode. I felt shame on its behalf, then on my own for having thought such a thing in the first place.

But gradually it grows on me. I have all but forgiven its inadvertent

lewdness and am adapting my expectations to accommodate its positive qualities. It may not be beautiful, but it certainly isn't boring. It may look top-heavy when seen from beside itself, but from the Town Bridge it looks stunning because the curve of the river moves it sideways so that it no longer overlaps the familiar contours of the existing bridges. And although it still looks like cranes from the pavement of John Frost Square, it looks genuinely magnificent from the roof of the art gallery.

And they will, won't they, touch up the paintwork where they damaged it in the process of erection? And put plasters on the grazes which are already weeping small runnels of rust? And surely they will finish taking the plastic wrapping from the great hawsers that join it all together? At the time of writing this is unravelling gradually like grave-windings on a skinny mummy, flapping and giggling in the wind.

WHO WERE THE CHARTISTS?

Here and there in the centre of Newport, the visitor will come up against mention of the Chartists. It is as well to know who they were, since they have been knitted into Newport's official history like an Aran cable.

Chartism was a working-class movement from 1839 to 1848. It arose like a rash all over Britain and was an attempt to establish parliamentary democracy by making sweeping changes to the political system of Britain and above all it wanted The Six Points (The Charter) introduced:

> 1. **Every man over twenty-one to have the right to vote**
> 2. **A secret ballot to be introduced**
> 3. **An MP did not have to own property of a certain value or above to become a MP**

4. All MP's to be paid to allow working men to serve in
Parliament
5. All constituencies to be equal in terms of population size
6. Elections to Parliament to be held every year so that MP's
would have to answer to their voters if they had not
performed well.

The leaders of the Chartists were a disparate group. There were
the militant tendency, like Feargus O'Connor and Wales's John Frost
who wanted to use force to get Parliament to accept the Charter.
Others, one William Lovett for instance, saw the movement as a
moral force and hoped to use more peaceful methods to persuade
Parliament to accept the changes. This mixture of persuasion and the
use of force did not make for strong leadership in the movement,
since the rank and file did not know which was the best direction to
take.

The loudest voice usually won and since nobody spoke out against
bully-boy Frost and his associates, they were able to summon up the
ragged army that marched on Newport in 1839. *(see: The Westgate)*

One of the methods used by the Chartists to persuade Parliament
was the collection of petitions. There were several countrywide
collections of signatures in the hope that Parliament would be
impressed with the number of people who supported the Chartists
and would push through what they perceived as popular change.
Petitions were collected in 1839, 1842 and 1848. The last of these had
five million signatures on it, but since one of them purported to be
that of Queen Victoria, it was obvious that there was skullduggery
afoot. The Chartist movement effectively collapsed thereafter.

But the Charter itself was basically a sound idea and five of the
Chartists' demands were eventually passed by Parliament and we now
take them for granted. Only the demand for an annual Parliament election
has never become law, for which we should all be profoundly grateful.

THE WESTGATE

Oh, what has happened to the Westgate, famed in the city's history as
the site of the massacre of the Chartist rioters who marched on it in
November 1839, when it was a mere town, to demonstrate against the
holding of prisoners.

A ragged army marches into battle
Urging each other on like naughty boys;
Whipped up by hooligans dressed up as cattle
And fortified with beer and empty noise.
So sure that justice blindly marches with them;
So sure they're right and therefore they will win.
They know life must have something more to give them
And brave as lions they roar from inn to inn.
The sound of broken boots and muttered stories
Echoing down an unadopted street.
Along the unlit road to promised glories
The ragged army marches to defeat.

This incident had begun in May, when a prominent member of the Chartist movement, Henry Vincent, was arrested for making seditious speeches. At Monmouth Assizes in August, he was jailed for a year. Angered, the Welsh Chartists began to resort to violence.

Newport's Chartist delegate John Frost had actually wanted a peaceful protest meeting and a dignified march on Newport, where Vincent's release would be demanded. He reckoned that on this occasion sheer force of numbers would win the day and he and his fellow organisers Zephaniah Williams and William Jones assembled between six thousand and seven thousand miners and ironworkers. But the peaceful march had suddenly become something quite different. Poor John, like the sorcerer's apprentice, had lost control of his servants. A group of shady *agents provocateurs* who wore cowskins as nominal disguises and called themselves 'Scotch Cattle' moved

among the marchers and stirred up militance. There was talk of other towns being captured, and even the declaration of a new republic.

The authorities knew all about this and arrested some more Chartists whom they held in the Westgate Hotel, guarded by a troop of twenty-eight soldiers. As the mob gathered outside, the order was given to fire into the crowd. Twenty were killed and fifty wounded. This has been viewed ever since as an atrocity – superior firepower being employed against men brandishing less sophisticated weaponry – and is now presented by history as martyrdom in a just cause.

While I have no problem with the cause – it was just and right and worth the winning – I do worry about the underlying assumptions of the Westgate incident. And the odds, *the odds*. For even if the whole seven thousand did not show up at the Westgate, even if the most conservative estimate (three thousand) is taken, the odds against the soldiers were still considerably more than a hundred to one.

Forty years later one hundred and forty five soldiers took on four thousand similarly-equipped darkfaced adversaries, odds here of less than thirty to one. But how does history see the victors of Rourke's Drift? Heroes to a man. Something other than objectivity is at work here, *n'est-ce pas?*

When I first came to Newport I was shown the famous 'bullet-holes' in the fat pillars at the entrance. Having run a farm for the previous twenty years, I was amazed to see that the holes had appeared exactly where a person hanging a gate might have drilled them. These pillars are now invisible during the hours of daylight, behind the locked wooden doors that protect the upstairs premises of Club Baltica, where at night the youth of Newport party. The riotous uprisings are now on the inside of the hotel, while the long-ago shenanigans outside are commemorated by some of Newport's strangest public art.

Outside the hotel, where Commercial Street turns into High Street, near the top of Skinner Street and the foot of Stow Hill stands a group of three statues created by Christopher Kelly in 1991 to commemorate the uprising. They are a strange group, taking their titles from the abstract nouns on the Chartist banner – *Energy, Prudence, Union*. So far, so good. But what the resulting artefacts have to do with Chartism is still a mystery to me, despite having spent much time on the green seat alongside them, letting their aura waft

over me along with the smell of coffee from Starbucks, which now occupies the ground floor of the hotel.

Energy is two naked chaps, back to back, with flags, standing on pile of bodies. *Prudence* is a montage of tools from which is arising what appears to be the top half of a bare-chested bishop with his crozier in one hand and a scythe in the other. At the other side, with his back to the bishop, stands a chap in a greatcoat, looking dischuffed. *Union* is a family who seem to be doing a moonlight flit, with mother and father carrying what appears to be a heavy box – but whether it's a week's groceries or the Ark of the Covenant is impossible to tell from the expressions on the faces.

The three groups are being observed dispassionately by an unnamed fourth; a pile of pigeons, one on top of the other, like the suitors in the *Thousand and One Nights* – the Mayor, the Chief of Police, the Vizier, the King and the Carpenter. They were tricked by a cunning ruse and ended up stacked in layers in a cupboard for days until the carpenter, who was on top, had to empty his bladder. So he piddled on the King, who piddled on the Vizier, who piddled on the policeman who piddled on the Mayor... Perhaps this is relevant.

THE DAVIES STATUE

Outside New Look stands the strangest of the city's public sculptures. A tall thin man, completely shrouded in clinging drapery, poses, hands on hips, in what appears to be the pelvic girdle of some antediluvian mammal upon which two bronze birds are sitting, staring. This is the statue commissioned by the Council to commemorate the poet W. H. Davies.

I was there on behalf of the *Argus* when, as the plaque says, Councillor Harry G. Jones unveiled it in 1990, the fiftieth anniversary of the poet's death. But how could anyone unveil a veiled statue? I saw the joke, but I didn't laugh.

I stood aghast, like the little boy in the fairy story, but this time the emperor was clothed when he should have been naked. While the ceremony stuttered round me like gunfire I was suddenly certain that it was all a terrible mistake. The standing figure should have been smooth and glowing like the bones and the birds. The sculptor, Paul Bothwell Kincaid, had made a generous likeness of Davies in clay, on a wire frame, and it was in his studio, wrapped in polythene sheet to prevent its drying out, awaiting the finishing touches.

But outside the Council howled with impatience. 1990 was almost over and the statue had to be in place by the end of December. I had a vision of the lorry arriving at the studio, a team of pantomime brokers men loading the wrapped figure arbitrarily aboard and whisking it off to the foundry where it was cast in bronze as it was while Kincaid slept innocently elsewhere, awaking later to a *fait accompli*.

But who would dare to blow the gaff? Not me, squire, not me.

Thirteen years later I am sitting on one of the new seats commemorating Newport's elevation to city status. Above me the shrouded figure looms, cold and sinister. In the folds of fabric at his feet puddles have formed. A dull pigeon with a deformed leg takes a quick swig of the dirty water. Davies would have liked that.

Nothing has happened in the interim to confirm my earlier vision of events, so I suppose I must accept that this is how the piece was truly conceived. A sort of numb disappointment persists, a need to ask why. Davies answers:

> What prompted this you'll never know –
> Perhaps the artist hated me.

BARCLAYS BANK

Newport can be a rough old town. In 1739 John Wesley passed through here on his mission to Wales. He stopped off in Westgate

Square to preach and noted in his diary for the 19th October that he found the citizens of Newport the most insensible, ill-behaved people he had ever seen. Even today it is perhaps not always the easiest of places for a vulnerable woman to walk the streets alone, especially after the shops are shut and the hoodies roam the echoing streets. According to the GLC (Goldie Lookin Chain) Dictionary and Reference Guide, the streets of Newport on a Friday and Saturday night are spoken of as the Killing Fields and are known as the after-dark territory of the Valley Commandoes (youths from the Valleys, on the pull, identified by the toothbrushes in their shirt pockets).

I confess, though, that I have seldom felt especially threatened. Just occasionally. By awareness of cultural differences, for instance. By the weather and by the mud. And once by Barclays Bank.

I was trundling down Commercial Street on my way to the library to look up the Lyceum or some such, when it occurred to me that I was in need of a chequebook. I went into the branch, joined the queue for a cashier and, while I was waiting, I sorted out my debit card with all the details on it, including my married name. When the call came – *Cashier Number Seven, Please* – I dropped it into the well in front of her and asked politely if I might order a "cheque book for this current account?" She looked at the card and then at me, but instead of simply keying the request into her computer terminal as I had expected, she said that I would have to speak to 'a co-ordinator'. I looked for some sign as to where I should go next. "Just go and stand at in the reception area and someone will come," she said. Almost at once a very small lady detached herself from the shadow of a display board and came over to me. "What was it you wanted?" she said. I supposed the cashier had somehow alerted her. I handed her my debit card. "A cheque book for this current account", I said. She looked at it carefully for a while then said, very slowly, "You're not a *local* lady, Mrs. Gray".

This was a statement, not a question. "In what way?" I asked. Was it my accent? My appearance? "This sort code" she said, with exaggerated interest, "Where is it from?" She stretched her eyes and put her head on one side. I began to feel uneasy. "Brynmawr," I said. "My branch is in Brynmawr." "And have you ever had a cheque book for this account before?" she asked, *rallentando*. "Yes," I began, but got no further. "I'm going to have to ask you to wait to speak to someone else who can help you…"

I began to panic. I had only half an hour before the library closed. What was she suggesting? Did I not look like a respectable widow whose mites were in their safekeeping? Obviously not. The old flat shoes, the mudsplashed trousers, the ancient dufflecoat pulled awry by the lumpy backpack: I was obviously an opportunist bagwoman. I had probably found or stolen the card. "Thanks – I'll leave it..." I said, took the card and ran for the door, half convinced a shutter would descend to trap me. Out of the door, down the steps, turn left and run...

As I did so I felt my right knee protest and turn to jelly. I felt myself begin to fall. The rucksack unbalanced me, I reached out, flailing, expecting the pavement to rise and claim me, to land in a grazed heap at the feet of a few embarrassed observers.

But surprisingly I did not hit the ground. I carried on at forty-five degrees to the footway almost as far as the left turn into Austin Friars, with the underground toilets on the way to John Frost Square. I turned left. Straightening myself up I checked to see if I was being followed, then looked critically at my reflection in one of the shop windows. It was a hairdressers, called Elbow Room. Strange that, I thought to myself. How many people have hairy elbows?

THE BELL CARRIER

Getting my breath back, I find myself at the feet of a mighty bull. Not, however, in the sweaty throes of some some backstreet *corrida*, but in one of the approaches to John Frost Square. It is a pleasing statue of the beast that supposedly led St Woolos to found the first church on Stow Hill which stands, proud and patient, between the underground

lavvies (which close at five-thirty) and the scary tunnel with the Chartist mosaic. Called *The Bell Carrier*, this is one of the sculptures produced for Newport by Sebastien Boyesen during his tenure as Town Sculptor in 1993-1994. Boyesen's work is recognisably representational and has a slight touch of knowing *levitas* that endears it to the public at large. In all the years I've known this statue, I've never seen it defaced or disrespected. I think the sheer size and gentle power of the beast intimidates the riff-raff.

CHARTIST TOWER

Here, near *The Bell Carrier*, at the end of Upper Dock Street, where John Frost Square interposes itself between it and Lower Dock Street, stands Chartist Tower, Newport's tallest building. It's bloody huge. A great rectangular prism, the antithesis of the busy confections of the eighties with their cheerul exoskeletons of lifts and staircases and pipes. It houses the Crown Prosecution Service, but *not* the Passport Office, as a notice on the door sees fit to point out. The Passport Office is in Upper Dock Street too. But *not here*.

Chartist Tower is a serious, purposeful sort of end-in-itself; a substantial, even brutal exterior that makes a virtue of having no discernible innards, either. Staff at the Reference Library tell me that it was finished in 1968 but are unable to tell me why or by whom. Their collective recollection is that it once housed Her Majesty's Inland Revenue, but whether it was purpose-built for the extraction of taxes they are not able to say for sure. If it were, though, this might explain its unremittingly punitive appearance. I first went there in the mid-nineties, as the lesser of two evils. I was signing on as unemployed and claiming job seeker's allowance. I reported fortnightly to the job centre on my lack of success.

Waiting to Sign On

When we were very young our jobs were done
In potties, to rounds of adult applause.
Jobs done at the right time, in the right place,
Were suitably rewarded. In such soil
The Protestant work ethic germinated
And jobs done otherwhere or not at all
Were little milestones on the road to Hell.

The same attitude is apparent here
Where those without employment come to make
Their regular excuses. *No, not yet.*
I have done everything that you suggest

But had no luck so far. I'm really sorry.
And cap in hand we shuffle to the desk
To sign our little testaments of failure.

The ambience conspires to convince us
Our failure to perform is our own fault.
We are not giving out what is expected of us.
We are furballs in the innards of society.
We could all do jobs if we could be bothered
To straighten up and fly right. We're not trying
Hard enough. Not pushing. Not concentrating.

No longer a matter of self-esteem
Or of gainful employment; Job just is.
A word that doesn't stand for anything.
It bears no relation to skill or aptitude.
It has been bandied back and forth until
Its shades of meaning have been worn away
By constant successions of sweaty hands.

Here Job is once more what it used to be.
The word drops audibly from time to time
Breaking the surfaces of conversations
That trickle anonymously behind closed doors.
Stand in the queue and listen. You will hear it
Plopping disconsolately at random intervals –
Job. Job-job-job. Job. Job.

I was sent for a weeklong course of intensive training in jobseek-
ing, where I was taught to sell myself over the telephone and
persuaded to draw pictures of the hurdles I felt I had to overcome. I
did the first badly and the second a little too well, to judge by the
reactions of the organisers. But worse than this was being forced to
attend what was called (and spelled) JobClub.

At first this happened on Thursdays in Brynmawr Rugby Club. A
man in tan faux leather slip-on shoes asked me if I had a CV. I replied
with a smile that it would be impossible to have got to my age without
one and he said "Can I see it?" I offered to give him a brief summary
and he said he wanted to "see it". I said I did not have the written
details to hand and he said, scornfully "How can you apply for jobs
if you haven't got anything in writing?" I explained that I summarised

my life afresh each time, according to the job I was applying for and he seemed to think that this amounted to sharp practice. When he asked me what I 'did' and I said I was a writer, the scorn was spread so thickly over his face that I could see it mantle like rancid butter when he spoke. "So you think you're a bit of an arty type, do you?"

Then he did that thing with his head, giving it a smirky little sideways tip, then drawing the nostrils towards the eyebrows on little invisible strings. "Have you ever had anything – *published?*" and the "p" of "published" bounced off the shiny walls like a squash ball. I gave him a list. He was not impressed. There was no work for writers. My expensive MA in teaching creative writing did not count as a qualification and I was told I would have to retrain for one of the available jobs for middle-aged women without skills. It was either 'caring' for those unable to take care of themselves (I wouldn't have minded that at all, but was told I couldn't do it because I didn't have a driving licence) or making myself ready for one of the thousands of new jobs about to be created in Newport. A Korean conglomerate in the electronics field was opening a new factory and nobody in the Valleys would ever be without a job again. I was told I'd be taught circuit-welding in Ebbw Vale and if I refused I would be automatically denied further benefits.

I went to sign on and told them I'd rather stick pins in my eyes than work for LG and was prepared to sign off at once, but the lady there said there was one last chance and so I agreed to attend the Executive JobClub, in Newport. In Chartist Tower. This was how I came to know its sparse insides quite intimately and to hate the whole edifice with a passion.

The JobClub was on the thirteenth floor and I couldn't find any stairs. I was told there were none and I must use the lift. I couldn't quite believe this and said I was perfectly prepared to use service stairs. The uniformed bouncerman said firmly "No Stairs" and I thought of going home, but since the alternative was to sit on a production line at LG I gave in and used the lift. I knew I could never work for a company called Lucky GoldStar. It even had the internal Uppercase that I hated in the JobClub. Who would buy a product with such a label? And did they have a staff leisure facility and was it called the Joy Luck Club, I wondered.

But the huge site, subsidised by the government, was growing at an exponential rate on the Cardiff Road, and took up all the space between Cleppa Park and St Mellons. It was called Celtic Lakes and had a couple of real lakes to give it credibility and even a swan or two on fine days. LG was the future. Everybody said so.

The Executive JobClub was not all that much different from that dedicated to Other Ranks. Those who ran it were offhand and *laissez-faire*. But here the newspapers were broadsheets and we were allowed to use the computers ourselves. And we could make tea.

And there *were* stairs. I found a doorway onto them by turning right on leaving the JobClub entrance. True, they didn't go into the grubby vestibule of Chartist Tower. They led into the area behind the counter of the restaurant in British Home Stores, but I used them regularly and if anybody noticed, they didn't appear to mind.

One day recently I went into the newsagent opposite Chartist Tower to buy my occasional *Argust*. And from its front page I learned that LG had finally pulled out the last of its interests from the sad remains of Celtic Lakes, where grubby rubbish floats on the water where the swans used to be. I realised sadly that I had seen a whole chapter open and close and that I was somehow more bound up in the story of Newport than I had hitherto supposed.

JOHN FROST SQUARE

The tourist information office, the main library, the art gallery and the mechanical clock that was the wonder of the Ebbw Vale Garden Festival; all these are to be found in John Frost Square.

John Frost was the leader of the Chartist uprising in Newport which threatened to result in a nationwide revolution. He was a prosperous businessman who had been jailed for libel in a dispute over his uncle's will. He blamed his uncle's solicitor Thomas Prothero for William Foster's decision to exclude him from the legacy. He was told that if he kept on pestering Prothero he would be jailed again, so he decided to turn his vitriolic attentions towards one of Prothero's friends, local landowner Sir Charles Morgan. He wrote a pamphlet accusing Sir Charles of mistreating his tenants and calling for free elections as the only way of curbing the power of the ruling classes. He became a political activist and a popular figure, and was one of Newport's first Councillors. He was soon appointed a magistrate and elected Mayor.

This, as it turned out, was not a Good Idea and he was quickly replaced as Mayor because of his aggressive behaviour. He began campaigning for the People's Charter for electoral reform, and was sacked as a magistrate for advocating violence.

In 1838 the arrest and conviction of fellow Chartist Henry Vincent, the 'Demosthenes of the West', for making inflammatory speeches and his subsequent committal to Monmouth Jail fuelled a wave of violence and Frost toured the nation calling for a massive protest against Vincent's imprisonment.

On 4th November 1839, Frost arrived in Newport with at least three thousand marchers to find that the authorities had arrested and were holding several Chartists at the Westgate Hotel *(qv)*. Soldiers inside the building opened fire on the protesters, killing twenty-odd and wounding fifty. Frost and his fellow protest leaders were found guilty of high treason and were actually sentenced to be hanged, drawn and quartered.

However, the Government wavered at the thought of what might happen should the punishment be carried out and, on the 1st February 1840, the sentences were commuted to transportation to Australia for life, Frost being sent to Tasmania where he worked as a clerk and a school teacher. After eleven years in exile Frost was granted a pardon in 1854 but initially forbidden to return to Britain. He spent the next two years touring the United States lecturing on the unfairness of the

British Government, which may have persuaded the authorities to relent and allow him to return to Britain where he was hailed a hero. His final years were spent writing in support of electoral and penal reform until he died 1877 at the age of ninety-three.

THE NEWPORT CLOCK

This is actually rather fun. It's thirty feet high and looks like a steel model of the *Arc de Triomphe* with a clock on it. It was originally built to represent Newport at the Ebbw Vale Garden Festival.

The Garden Festivals were a short-lived phenomenon. Based on the *Bundesgartenschau*, introduced in post-war Germany to bring war-damaged areas back into use, the concept was first mooted as a regeneration tool by former Environment Secretary Michael Heseltine in 1980. A programme of five festivals was devised, to be held biennially in Stoke-on-Trent, Glasgow and Gateshead, starting with Liverpool and ending with Ebbw Vale. Each festival took a derelict piece of land, reclaimed it and turned it into green space for the event. While the festivals only lasted for one summer, it was hoped they would encourage investment and development long afterwards.

Ebbw Vale is a small town at the head of one of the valleys above Newport. It has its own small river, which runs down to join the Usk south west of the city. Its rugby team is still defiantly known as The Steelmen despite the industry that was its lifeblood having been taken away bit by bit. It was on the site of the main steelworks, which closed in 1970, that the Garden Festival of Wales took place in 1992. The nearby Marine Colliery, also closed, was turned into a huge car park.

I applied for the position of events officer but I was clearly not up to it. I was asked to design an opening ceremony. The lady who interviewed me told me that one of their applicants had proposed floating a grand piano on a raft down the river, complete with lighted candles and a Liberace lookalike. Genuinely interested, I asked if they had actually seen the river and what plans they had for the supermarket trolleys and sewage outlets. And the bit where it goes through the culvert under the rolling mill? Would Liberace dismount or duck? I think my scepticism lost me the job.

Late Submission

An idea for an opening event for the Ebbw Vale Garden Festival.

How about this one, then; this one has everything –
A real Welsh focus, lots of local jobs –
It even, in the long term, saves you money.

An all-round winner. This is what you do.
Instead of tarting-up the area
And planting bloody daffodils in rows
All through that little town the Yanks call "quim";
Instead of pulling down the old Marine
And turning it into a parking space,
Leave it alone until the opening night;
Leave all the loose coal and the winding gear
And make it look as if it's still a go.
Then, when you get the punters through the gates,
Say your piece, cut the tape – and blow it up!
You'd have to look into the safety thing,
Of course, and have a word with Equity.
Nothing the PR people couldn't handle.
An instant pit disaster! Lovely stuff!
The Fire Department could mount a display –
And what a showcase for the Gwent Police!
You could pay signers-on to limp about
And local women could dress up and weep.
The thing has endless possibilities.
You could sell bits of it as souvenirs
For the duration of the Festival.
Go on. This one's a winner. Ask yourselves:
Who in the great wide world would miss a chance
To watch somebody else's tragedy.

The Garden Festival opened on 1st May and ran until the end of September. "A long, long time" as the Kurt Weill song has it. Local authorities provided individual showpieces. Blaenau Gwent, the host authority, had contrived a brave and beautiful exhibit – a piece of neglected narrow-gauge track with a rusting coal-dram, planted with wildflowers of the sort that appear spontaneously to smooth the ugly face of dereliction. It is one of the only two exhibits I can still call to mind. The other one being Newport's clock; one of the few that survived and still pleases the punters. When it's working, that is.

Now it has its permanent home here in John Frost Square. Its creator, Andy Plant, describes it as a cross between a cuckoo clock and an espresso machine. Every hour, on the hour, it does its stuff. Skeletons pop out of the top, smoke oozes from the cracks, several tons of steel come apart and open up to reveal the angel mechanics who live inside it. They are fast asleep. A cuckoo wakes them. They get up in a panic and set to work like blazes, rewinding the clock weight, while the whole structure puts itself back together again, ready for the next hour. At first people used to gather round to watch it, but then it seemed to be taken for granted and the last time I passed it there was a notice to say it was out of order. Should it still be so – and it probably is – turn your back to it and look up at the library.

THE MUSEUM AND LIBRARY

This building has one of the most surprising frontages in Newport. Huge, bright and inventive, showing up the drab shopfronts around the square for a row of unimaginative concrete boxes. Inside, too, it is pleasingly suited to its main purposes – an impressive and helpful library, an adequate if predictable museum and an art gallery that now and again exceeds all expectations.

It has other, subsidiary purposes. A Tourist Information Office on the ground floor selling the sort of tat that tempts impecunious children and two wide, glass-surrounded landings that are home during opening hours to groups of streetwise Asian lads, whose implausibly white trainers make nonsense of the implications of their expensive sportswear. They hang out happily here, provided they do not breach the three cardinal rules laid down by the lady in Information. They do not swear, they do not smoke (though they may go out into the square and come back in again) and they do not diss the visiting citizens. They have come to an accommodation; their figures in the windows, arses against the glass, are like living sculptures, an installation that constantly changes yet remains always in place.

The museum houses the expected exhibits formed by spin-offs from local history, the highlights in this case being the Roman artefacts from Caerwent, the collection of Chartist memorabilia and the haphazard accumulation of ships' bits from the great days of maritime trade. It is a museum where it is safe to have favourite things. You can come to visit them on a whim at any time, knowing that they will be there, just where you left them.

Mind you, there are the occasional one-offs. A natural history display – the garden at dawn – with lots of stuffed animals. As you creep up on it the light comes on, to catch the night visitors off guard. Dusty little rodents with faraway boot-button eyes and birds frozen crisp and stiff somewhere between life and art, caught in the act of falling off their perches. All of them, I felt, looked a little sorry for themselves.

They recently had a special display related to the Royal Ordnance Factory no.11, which operated in Newport throughout World War Two. This included several contemporary works of art, including a copy of Laura Knight's "Ruby Loftus screwing a breech ring", which was painted at the factory in the forties. The title so appealed to me, albeit for all the wrong reasons, that I sought further information and discovered that Ruby Loftus was a lathe operator who had been trained to thread the breech ring of the Bofors gun. This was a particularly delicate operation, thought impossible for a woman to do. Ruby showed 'em…

Of girls and guns...

(after Henry Reed)

> To-day we have naming of parts. Yesterday,
> We had daily cleaning. And to-morrow morning,
> We shall have daily cleaning again. But to-day,
> To-day we have naming of parts. *Ruby Loftus*
> Glistens like gunmetal among all the neighbouring workers
> And to-day we have naming of parts.

This is the QF 40 mm Mark I. All it needs
Is conversion from metric to imperial. As you will see
The parts are designed for hand assembly
And are labelled "file to fit". Ruby Loftus
Flexes her forearms in silent, eloquent gestures
Designed for hand assembly.

This is the breech-ring, which is always screwed
With a steady turn of the wrist. And please do not let me
See any girl using her fingers. You can do it quite easy
If you have any strength in your wrist. Ruby Loftus
Works, swift and meticulous, never letting anyone see
The slightest suspicion of fingers.

This is the Kerrison Predictor. The purpose of this
Is to drive the laying electrically. You point at the target,
Dial in the range and atmospheric conditions
And the gunners just load the clips. Ruby Loftus
Imagines herself laid electrically, screwing the breech ring
In atmospheric conditions.

This is a Stiffkey Stick, which is pronounced "stookey"
So don't anybody say anything. The back-up sights
Are ring-and-post, replacing the old reflectors
Which in our case we have not got. Ruby Loftus
Dreams of doing her bit with a stiff key stick
For to-day we have naming of parts

The art gallery is on the third floor. "The art gallery presents exhibitions, educational activities and houses collections of historic and contemporary British paintings. Of particular note is the John Wait teapot display and the Fox collection of decorative art." (I got that from the guidebook I picked up in Tourist Information).

My own favourite thing in the art gallery is Jacob Epstein's bust of W.H. Davies. Epstein cast six of these and the impecunious and thrifty Davies asked if he might purchase one for the price of the metal. Epstein let him have it for a tenner. Davies loved that bust, which later gave rise to a poem.

Works of Art

When I went wandering far from home
I left a woman in my room
To clean my hearth and floor, and dust
My shelves and pictures, books and bust.

When I came back a welcome glow
Burned in her eyes – her voice was low;
And everything was in its place
As clean and bright as her own face.

But when I looked more closely there
The dust was on my dark, bronze hair;
The nose and eyebrows too were white –
And yet the lips were clean and bright.

The years have gone, and so has she,
But still the truth remains with me –
How that hard mouth was once kept clean
By living lips that kissed unseen.

When I first came here in search of the famous likeness, I asked an attendant where the bust was to be found. I was not even certain that it was in the gallery. I had seen pictures of it but had not been able to establish its exact whereabouts. The man looked thoughtful, then frowned exaggeratedly. "I'm not sure," he said. "Perhaps…" and he laid his hand on my shoulder and steered me into the next room. Gently he turned me round and I stood face to face with the old rogue himself. "I'll leave the two of you together," said the attendant, grinning.

There he was, with his ugly face and his ridiculous quiff, smiling impudently. I didn't lean over and kiss him on the lips, though, partly because his shelf was a little too high and I'd have triggered an alarm, but more importantly because I was aware of the closed circuit cameras watching my every move. Notwithstanding, I did place a surreptitious kiss on the tip of a finger, which I then slid lightly along his bronze grin. When I examined the finger afterwards there was no trace of dust. Someone else had been there first.

I trusted the art gallery to keep faith, like the museum, but in this I was deceived. On my most recent visit to the gallery I found a new exhibition being hung. The teapots were still there, dammit, but Willy Davies's shelf was empty. He is now, I was told, in storage. I can still visit him, but only by appointment. Who will dust him now?

THE KINGSWAY CENTRE

Kubla Kingsway

Or, A Vision in a Dream

In Newport once did Kubla Khan
A shapeless shopping mall decree
Where Usk the mighty river ran
O'er broken bike and three-wheeled pram
   Into the Estuary.
And many miles of retail space
Were fitted out and filled apace
And there were basements bright with budget ware
Where bubbled many an incense-burning ring
And there were innovations everywhere
Embracing little bits of everything.
But Oh! the marble staircase steep which slanted
Down to the ground athwart the mezzanine
Whereon the public, gobsmacked and enchanted,
With sumptuous stock bedazzled, bargain-haunted,
Sailed up and down, unhassled and serene,
While from below there rose a ceaseless sighing
As though all Wales its vast thick pants were buying.
For miles meandering with a mazy motion
Besotted shoppers through sweet perfumes threaded
And each toward their chosen counter headed
To test the efficacy of the latest lotion;
Inhaling ecstasy from tube and jar

And leaving even lovelier than before.
The shadow of this place of pleasure
Fell like a blessing on the town
And from it came the jingling measure
Of honest trading going down.
It was a miracle of rare device,
This place of promissory merchandise.

There came a cry: Beware! Beware!
And through the sacred halls there strode
A burly bloke who bore a load
Of plastic garden furniture
And bellowed for a signature.
I never knew the dullard's name
Only that the consignment came
From Porlock... *O-o-oh... bollocks...*

KINGSWAY CAR PARK

Rod Liddle wrote in the *Sunday Times*:

> The late novelist Rayner Heppenstall once spent a few months in a
> blindfold, walking around Newport, Gwent. There are quite a few
> British towns one might better experience without actually having to
> see them, and Newport, I reckon, falls into that category.

I shrugged, and looked into the matter. Heppenstall met his future
wife Margaret Edwards at a literary gathering in 1936 and they
married in Newport, because it was her home town, in 1937. Most of
his published poetry was written during this period but now he
wished to write a novel, and to write it from the point of view of a
sightless masseur. Hence the blindfold. The book, however, wasn't set
in Newport but in Cornwall and the worst excesses of urban desce-
cration had not been perpetrated upon the town at that time, so I am
inclined to believe that his reasons had more to do with artistic
authenticity than aesthetic denial.

Liddle continues:

> a noble and imaginative idea, I think you will agree. Trouble is, the
> book, *The Blaze of Noon*, is pretty poor. Rayner seems to have been so

wrapped up in being a blind person that he forgot to make the story either interesting or meaningful.

Although published in 1939 and condemned as obscene by the *London Evening Standard*, it was, arguably, the first example of the *nouveau roman* later developed by Robbe-Grillet, Sarraute and Duras. 'Interesting' and 'Meaningful' became, for a while, suspect criteria; I was much taken with the genre in my impressionable teens. In fact my own translation of a Duras novella, ribbon-typed on quarto paper, lies in the canterbury within reach of my right hand. The staples have almost rusted away. The title is *Les Chantiers* – The Building Site. This is interesting but not meaningful.

Heppenstall got his title from Milton's Samson Agonistes – 'O, dark, dark, dark amid the blaze of noon' – but while his protagonist, Louis Dunkel, progresses the narrative by feeling up the daughter of the house, Samson, enraged and inwardly enlightened, literally brings it down.

And today the mighty bulldozers struck the first killing blow to the greatest blemish in the city centre – the Kingsway car-park is no more! I am punching the sky with an enormous 'Yes!' Perhaps it is still too soon to ask the likes of Mr Liddle to take off his metaphorical blindfold, but as that hideous pile of filthy concrete collapses at last on the heads of the aesthetically unsighted, I feel in my water that it won't be long. Today the multi-storey – tomorrow the bus station. Go, Newport! – you can do it!

THE DOLMAN THEATRE

The Dolman Theatre, on Kingsway, has a brand new face, which has been put on where its arse used to be; an interesting concept you'll agree.

I first came across the Dolman as the meeting place of the Gwent Poetry Society, a group which it has been my pleasure to address annually

for many years. They meet in one of the upstairs rooms among props and flats and furnishings, all set about with *trompe l'oeil* doors and windows that give access to imaginary woods and pastures new. It looked and felt and smelt like a working theatre. I'm glad to say it still does, despite its new façade.

For as long as I've known it, the entrance to the theatre was via the main hall of the Kingsway Shopping Centre. All that could be seen from the main road was the great cliff of puce brickwork that formed its unsavoury backside, with a small stage door lurking up an alley.

It was always a bit depressing, turning up early for a workshop or a reading and standing about in the empty shopping mall, wandering across from time to time to stand with my face pressed against the glass doors, watching people inside going about their business. The new aspect is a huge improvement. I hope it will help the Dolman not to feel too threatened by the new Riverfront Arts Centre which can be seen from its fine new doorstep.

Although the present theatre was born in the sixties, its governing body, the Newport Playgoers, has been active in am-dram since its foundation in 1924. Plays were put on in various available venues, but when the membership swelled to an impressive five hundred in 1933, local solicitor Arthur Dolman proposed the formation of a Building Committee to work towards a proper theatre of their own. The Newport Little Theatre Company was floated and the sale of shares in it produced enough money to buy a disused church in Dock Street, which was converted and opened as The Little Theatre in 1937.

Two years later the war came and the theatre was in danger of closure or – perhaps worse – military requisition. The canny president, Tom Webley, became Entertainments Officer to the troops stationed in the Newport and formed the 'Flashlights' concert party, and the theatre remained open for the performance of plays to the troops and nursing units. Like London's Windmill, it remained open all through the war.

The Little Theatre flourished, but so did Newport. In 1960 work commenced on the new Spencer Steelworks at Llanwern and the town was considered ripe for development once again. A property development company – Sovereign Securities – started scouring Newport for likely sites for investment and the Little Theatre and its adjoining properties were just the sort of thing they were looking for. The Little Theatre Company owned the freehold of a large chunk of Dock Street and Sovereign made them an offer they thought they couldn't refuse. But refuse they did.

Clever Arthur Dolman explained that the company didn't want money; they wanted a theatre. Sovereign Securities agreed to build a new theatre to the Company's specification in return for all the Dock Street properties. This witty little game of Monopoly allowed both sides to win and the Dolman Theatre opened its back-to-front doors in 1967. In the lower foyer are all the old gargoyles, rescued from the Little Theatre and the new mural painted by Hans Feibusch (who else?) who was much in demand after his work in the Civic Centre.

THE MARKET HALL

One of the loveliest buildings in Newport is the old market hall, but it's hard to stand back far enough from it to see how fine it is. It is marooned in a welter of little fiddled-with streets between the bus and railway stations. Plans are afoot to make it a greater feature of the city, but please God it will be done by different hands than those who have 'improved' the inside of it.

Once upon a time it was a great, high-ceilinged hall with a breathtaking roof supported by soaring steel barrel-vaulting exactly mirroring Brunel's mighty Paddington Station and equally worthy of protection and respect. Victorian architecture and industrial know-how making each other magnificent. That was how I remembered it. You could stand tall and tip your head back, staring into echoing

space around the edge of which ran a magical gallery. Up there the loucher element of the merchant-tenants offered their wares. Hippy artefacts, underground comics and scented candles. And books. Troutmark Books. I loved the sign above the burgeoning stall: TROUT-MARK BOOKS. LONDON – PARIS – NEW YORK – NEWPORT. Now that's style!

Now Troutmark trade downstairs and it doesn't feel the same. In fact the whole hall is different; dark, oppressively humid and acoustically ugly. This is because the area previously encircled by the gallery has been filled in and the great vaulted ceiling is no longer visible from the ground floor. Upstairs the central area is now a sort of unfortunate café, with a floor made of wood and dysfunctional glass on which ice cream wrappers and pale undead chips accumulate and adhere heartlessly until closing time. A botched loft conversion that should never have been passed by the planners. I hate it. May it collapse without loss of life in the middle of the night.

Outside, Sebastien Boyesen's peasant pig pauses with its basket of produce. Light glints on the adorable snout that has been buffed to a high polish by thousands of affectionate rubs and twice as many surreptitious touches-for-luck by passers-by. It stands looking wistfully at the building, wondering, like the rest of us, what will happen next.

BELLE VUE PARK

I had been saving the park for one of the visits in the company of my dog, Otis, but it is not a dog-friendly park. There are notices insisting on leads at all times, so I explored it on my own, wishing often that he could have been with me.

The land on which Belle Vue Park stands was a gift to the town from Lord Tredegar in 1891 to provide a public park for the people of Newport. An open competition to design and construct the park was won by Thomas Mawson of Windermere (1861-1933) but the whole thing nearly ended in disaster. After Mawson's design had been approved and the contract awarded, he realised that he had in fact designed it for the neighbouring field, the site of the present Royal Gwent Hospital. Mawson, it seems, had misread the map on his first visit to Newport. It was a classic case of back to the drawing board and Mawson had to re-think his plans in a hurry, but the result was a great success and nobody regretted having given young Mawson his big chance.

Belle Vue Park was Thomas Mawson's first win in an open competition. He went on to become one of the foremost landscape architects of his time, responsible for the design of many gardens in his adopted Cumbria, including Holker Hall and Rydal Hall as well as Dyffryn Botanic Garden in Cardiff. In November 1892 Lord Tredegar performed the ceremony of cutting the first sod; construction began and the park opened on 8th September 1894. The final cost of the park is recorded as £19,500.

Following a successful bid to the Heritage Lottery Fund for considerably more than that, the park is undergoing restoration with the aim of recreating the original Edwardian planting scheme and restoring the buildings. The five-year project aims to retain and enhance the original character and features of the park. The idea is to provide a green open space, catering for modern needs while respecting the historic fabric and integrity of Mawson's design. Work began in May 2003 and should be completed by the end of 2006. But don't hold your breath; when I was there in May the old tearoom was still in prefabricated pieces on the ground. But it's well on the way.

Sadly, though, as one project draws to a close another cries for attention. The fine new gates have been attacked by vandals and are once again off for repair. *Plus ça change...*

Belle Vue Park had many features typical of a turn-of-the-century public space, including the conservatories and pavilion, bandstand and rockeries. The Cascade was an especially popular feature, which will be reinstated as part of the restoration. *The South Wales Argus* published this report on the day the park opened:

> There are a series of cascades, with two bridges of architectural design thrown across the stream, and when the ferns have established themselves, it will form a very delightful little dell.

Additional features were added to the park throughout the years.

The bowling greens were opened in 1904 and a Tea House added in 1910. In 1924 the adjoining house and grounds of Belle Vue House came into the Council's ownership and the additional eleven acres of land were absorbed into the park, which now extended to twenty-six acres.

The Gorsedd Stone Circle was erected in 1896, for the National Eisteddfod held here in 1897. It seems a small, sad little circle, not very far from a busy road, set among oak trees that have clearly grown a lot since it was new. But the most impressive tree in the vicinity is the mighty Weymouth Pine, which stands on the path that approaches the circle. Its constantly dropping needles crunch underfoot. Light filters through the high branches and the ground below is littered with huge cones, long and slightly bent, like the turds of some mythical beast that had moments earlier been snuffling for truffles under the tree. I tried the old challenge of counting the stones and couldn't come up with the same number twice, so I put one of the cones on one of the stones and started again. But then, when I got back to the cone-stone I couldn't remember whether that was 'one', or whether... you get my drift? I experimented till I got a number I was satisfied with (but I won't tell you what it was so you can have the fun of doing it for yourself) and then slipped the co-operative cone into my rucksack, where it oozed odoriferous sticky stuff all over my camera and notebook. Both still whiff slightly of municipal toilets.

The Weymouth Pine is one of very few of these trees outside Longleat, where it was first introduced by Lord Weymouth. In fact the park contains a number of rare specimens. In early spring the Himalayan Magnolias produce huge goblet-shaped pink flowers and when I was there the beautiful Judas Trees were covered with clusters of rose-lilac. In June and July the Tulip Tree produces its distinctive orange tulip-shaped blooms, but I missed those this year and had to take it on trust. But never mind, autumn brings strange colours, too; especially beautiful are the clear yellow leaves of Ginkgo Biloba, one of only four deciduous conifers that can be seen growing in the British Isles today, and the glorious crimson of the Liquidambar, a native of the eastern United States.

At the height of summer 2006 a telephone call to the park provided the latest update. The water was still not restored to the cascade but the electrics were in place, coupled into those of the pavilion, whose floor was being tiled as we spoke. It is difficult to marry the needs of the Lottery fund for value and accountability with those of CADW for excellence and authenticity and one set of tiles had been condemned on delivery for too great a variation in colour. Those in charge of the park are still excited by what it used to be and what it can become. Their enthusiasm is infectious.

During September 2005 a crew from BBC Wales visited the park to film a number of scenes for the second series of *Dr Who*. Other scenes were shot in the city centre and at Dyffryn. All of the Belle Vue scenes were filmed in and around the fountain bowl, near the bowling greens. It was not one of the better episodes. As well as David Tennant and Billie Piper, some scenes featured the dog K9, one of the sillier innovations from one of the earlier series. I noted with amusement that it was not on a lead and hoped at every moment that one of the marvellous staff would leap out from a bush and insist on its immediate removal.

WEST

THE MORGANS AND TREDEGAR HOUSE

One of the lines I followed when I was seeking material for this book was the life of Henry Morgan, pirate-turned-statesman. I had been told he came from Newport.

I had always imagined him as a charismatic eccentric with a wooden leg and a parrot on his shoulder. Now I saw him sailing forth from the mouth of the Usk to harry the Spaniard and trouser his doubloons. I eagerly sought details, only to find that I had been following a false lead and he had no real connection with Newport at all. He was born in 1635 in Llanrhymney, which was then "a manor in the hundred of Newport, Monmouthshire" but is now a suburb of Cardiff and towards the end of his life he is said to have bought an estate in Jamaica and named it Penkarne. And Pencarn was another of the manors in the Hundred of Newport (a 'hundred' being a subdivision of a county for administrative and taxation purposes, called in other parts of the country a leet, a ward or a wapontake).

He was a junior officer in Cromwell's army and was sent to Barbados on an expedition when he was twenty. He didn't come back to Britain except for a brief stay in London between 1672 and 1675 when he was brought back under arrest because of his buccaneering exploits against Spain, whose friendship was being sought by King Charles. However, when it became apparent that the Spanish alliance was a lost cause, the king knighted him and sent him back as Governor of Jamaica.

He never returned. And, bless him, he was more of a soldier than a sailor. His great victories were on land, his sea exploits often ending in disaster. One ship exploded beneath him when his crew, doubtless under the influence of grog, lit a lot of candles a bit too near the gunpowder store and on another occasion his ship struck a reef near shore and he had to be rescued from a rock.

However, John Weston, whose researches on the Morgan family I have plundered as shamelessly as Henry did the Spanish Main, ends his piece:

> For many, Henry Morgan is little more than the name of a romantic 'pirate' of yore, but I now see signs of Morgan being re-evaluated as one of Britain's most successful military strategists and as a man with the leadership qualities of an Alexander. He gained the loyalty of the buccaneers, who followed him without question, and the respect of kings and princes. Of all the great figures in Welsh history he must be counted among the most attractive and able.

And he was born 'according to some accounts' in the Hundred of Newport. Nice one. But he wasn't one of the Morgans of Tredegar House, the only stately home in Newport.

TREDEGAR HOUSE

This extraordinarily beautiful mansion once stood at the centre of an estate extending to a thousand acres of parkland. Gradually nibbled away by urban development and sliced-off suddenly by the M4, the park has been reduced to just ninety acres, but its lovely remains are supposedly safe at last from further encroachment.

Since the beginning of the fifteenth century, the estate was owned a branch of the Morgan family. The present grand house was built after the Civil War, incorporating part of the earlier medieval building. With the marriage of William and Blanche Morgan in 1661, not only was the splendid mansion completed with the help of her huge dowry, but also the joining of these two influential families made them a powerful force to reckon with over the next two hundred and fifty years.

Their fortunes flourished, their influence grew exponentially. The business ventures of the great entrepreneur Charles Gould Morgan made the family a force to be reckoned with throughout the eighteenth century. Charles's son expanded the commercial and industrial empire and established Newport as an important trade centre. However, like many self-made men who rose to prominence in the world of commerce, the Morgans desperately wanted a title. This has so many modern overtones that I feel a little diffident about looking too carefully at how it was achieved – but nevertheless they bagged a baronetcy in 1859. And in 1905 the second Baron, Godfrey Charles Morgan, who had taken part in the Charge of the Light Brigade at Balaclava, became the first Viscount Tredegar.

But from then on, it was all downhill for the Morgans. Having achieved greatness through social status and huge wealth, it was these very things that brought the family to ruin. Extravagance, eccentric pursuits and hefty death duties whittled away the family's assets over the next three generations. During this time the house was refuge to the wonderful Catherine Morgan, who believed herself to be a bird and built nests in the grounds. One of these was actually big enough for her to sit in but whether she ever hatched any chicks in it is not a matter of record.

The last Morgan to live in Tredegar House was Evan, who was

deeply interested in black magic and was known for his wild weekend parties attended by a curious mixture of the famous, the infamous and the merely interesting. Novelist Aldous Huxley, satanist Aleister Crowley – and the group of astonished ladies who are regarding him in a photograph taken around 1936, which shows him receiving guests in the gardens with his pet parrot 'Blue Boy' perched on his shoulder.

I was disappointed not to have been able to trace the pirate Henry Morgan to Tredegar House – but in Evan I found my charismatic eccentric who really did have a parrot. Pity about the wooden leg, although two out of three ain't bad.

In 1951, the house was stripped, the contents auctioned, and the estate sold. For twenty-three years it was used as a school but was finally purchased by Newport Borough Council in the 1970s. Since then it has been restored, bit by bit, to something suggesting its former grandeur. Although the majority of contents were scattered at the sale of the house, some have since been recovered and returned. The rare 'Tredegar Salt', a silver salt cellar inscribed with the Morgan family crest, was discovered at auction a few years ago and purchased for a staggering sum in order for it to be reinstated in the dining room. There was, as you can imagine, much complaining that the money could have been better spent.

I wanted to include a photograph of it, but was told by the front office that I couldn't take one without a special appointment. When I contacted the management to ask permission I was told that I would have to apply in writing and if it was to be for a commercial purpose – a book for instance – there would be a charge…

So I went to have a look at it, along with all the other punters, so as to describe it for you as best a poet may.

The Ballad of the Tredegar Salt

Oh, the Morgans of Tredegar, they were all but on the street
So they sold the family silver in a bid to make ends meet.
They sent the Salt to Sotheby's and fairly well it did,
But Newport Council bought it back for fourteen thousand quid.

I thought it would be marvellous, a wonder of the world;
Perhaps a golden galleon with silver sails unfurled,
All artfully constructed on a raft of little wheels
To trundle down the table during under-seasoned meals.

> But it's not the tarty artefact to which the rich aspire;
> It's a tiny little, shiny little object of desire.
> It's half a salt-and-pepper set, a pillar with a dome,
> Though marginally larger than the one I have at home.
>
> It's not at all spectacular; it's functional and neat
> And it teeters on the tablecloth on little ball-y feet.
> I don't know if the top comes off; I can't see how you fill it
> But since I shan't be asked to dine this will not matter, will it?
>
> Some say it's solid silver; some say it's parcel gilt
> But it serves a sterling purpose and ensures no salt is spilt.
> And it's altogether better than the greaseproof paper twists
> For which the gawpers grovel in their bags of noisy crisps...

Nobody knows for sure the actual designer or builder of Tredegar House but much of the exterior does *look* like the style of Inigo Jones. And the time-frame fits. Internally, the rooms have been restored as far as possible to an original condition, helped by old photographs and the grim inventories of bankruptcy. In the grounds are several old barns and outbuildings from various stages of its history and an unusually upmarket stable block that was quite clearly designed to be a miniature version of the house. There is a separate orangery, approached through a walled garden, which contains a stunning eighteenth century parterre created from an assortment of gravel, crushed shells and grass.

And, believe it or not, there is a caravan site for eighty pitches alongside one of the lakes. Good old Newport.

THE SAINT AND THE APOSTROPHE

If you ask anyone in Newport the name of the cathedral at the top of Stow Hill, they will tell you 'Saint Woolos'. They say *wooluss*, as though it rhymes with 'bullace' – the little wild plum that grows in the hedgerows. Or the exhortation to a cab-horse to 'pull us'. This fascinates me. Indeed, 'Saint Woolos Cathedral' is how it appears on the official leaflet.

But if the saint's name really is Woolos, surely the cathedral that is dedicated to him would be accorded an element of possession – like St Paul's or St David's – thereby becoming Saint Woolos's

(Woolusses)? Or, if the double 's' is awkward, Saint Woolos' with a soundless but perfectly visible apostrophe.

Me, though, I doubt the whole ethos of Woolos. It doesn't make sense. Research tells me that the W-word, whatever it is, is actually a corruption of his Welsh name, Gwynllyw, by thick-tongued foreign invaders who could only reproduce an approximation of the sound. As a person of this persuasion, I have experimented endlessly.

Woolo (pronounced *wool-oh?*) makes sense; I can make it out of Gwynllyw fairly easily, especially after a glass or two of something. However, no way can I summon up an 's' to top it off with. Why would a busy barbarian bother? Unless, of course, the terminal 's' was added by these language bandits to express their own hamfisted genitive. And, this being the case, should it not be preceded by an apostrophe? Saint Woolo's. No need to change the sound, just the appearance, so it doesn't look weird.

It bothers me, but apparently it doesn't matter tuppence to the people of Newport, who, as is pointed out elsewhere, have an idiosyncratic approach to language. So – when in Rome, as it were…

Let us just assume that the saint has somehow swallowed his own apostrophe. Or perhaps he simply offloaded it onto St. Michael, who has special responsibility for greengrocers.

SAINT WOOLOS THE BLOKE

The usual version of the story runs as follows: St Gwynllyw Farfog, *(The Bearded)* was King of Lowlands on the west side of the Usk around AD 466-523. He was known in Latin as Gundleus and in English as Woolos.

Gwynllyw had his eye on Gwladys, the daughter of his neighbour Brychan, the King of Brecknock. He did the decent thing first of all, sending a message requesting her hand in marriage, but Brychan gave a dusty answer so Gwynllyw decided to abduct her and with the help of a warband of three hundred, he raided Brecknock and took her. She was to remain with him for the rest of his life.

Brychan gave chase and they all met up with King Arthur, who fancied Gwladys himself but was persuaded to side with Gwynllyw and did that Arthur-thing with the usual effect. Brychan was immediately persuaded that it was a good idea after all and gave his blessing.

Gwynllyw's dodgy dealings continued. After the birth of his eldest son (Cadoc, or Cadfael), he wetted the baby's head copiously, then went on a wild celebratory raid on Gwent with his fearless warband. He helped himself to lots of other people's livestock, including a cow belonging to the Irish saint Tathyw of Caerwent, who promptly arrived at Gwynllyw's court and demanded it back. The king would not let the cow go however, until Tathyw had baptised his new-born son into the Christian faith. So Tathyw led his cow back to Caerwent and left behind the makings of a saint.

Gwynllyw and Gwladys continued their wild ways. They are said to have practised cold water bathing in the Usk all year-round, preceded and followed at night by a mile-long walk in the nude. Cadoc, it is said, despaired of them. Then a strange thing happened. Gwynllyw had a dream in which a heavenly messenger appeared and told him he would find a beautiful white ox – far better than Tathyw's cow – at the top of the hill the rose up from the river. Stow Hill as we know it now.

Up he trudged – and there it was! The king was so impressed that he allowed Cadoc to convert both himself and his wife to Christianity. He then founded the Church of St Mary (now St Woolos' Cathedral) where the ox was found.

Another version of the story is that researched by Bernard Cornwell for his *Warlord* trilogy; yet another take on the Arthur legend. Here he appears under his Latin name, as Gundleus, king of the Silurians, one of the goriest baddies of the Dark Ages and Gwladys is a warrior maiden who rides at his side. Although Cornwell has him skewering the wetnurse's child in mistake for baby Mordred and poking out the eye of Merlin's legendary lover Nimue, this only emphasises the power of the teller of tales, who always has a hidden agenda. And anyway, is it any less feasible than the white ox option?

The storyteller in me lusts after a truth of my own. What if young Cadoc, clever little chap, planted the beast on Stow Hill and watched from behind a bush along with his friend Finian, stuffing their cassock-sleeves in their mouths to stifle the giggles as the fuddled old king wrestled with the concept of a holy miracle?

UP STOW HILL

Newport is not only a city – it is a Cathedral City. With a passing nod to Colonel Sanders on my right and Starbucks on my left, I start the not inconsiderable climb in search of its seat of ecclesiastical excellence. I set off up Stow Hill. Lesser churches, locked and wary, watch my progress.

I know from the tourist leaflet what it is I am supposed to find. St Woolos Cathedral dates back to the twelfth century but is built on a site that has been a place of worship since the sixth century when Prince Gwynllyw – the mysterious Woolos – built his mud and wattle church on it. Circa 800, Gwynllyw's church was replaced by a stone structure on the same site. Signs of this Saxon church remain in the Lady Chapel. In the eleventh century the church was attacked and left in ruins by pirates. *(Aha! See 'The Pirate and the Pill!)* The present building is of Norman origin and the arched entrance and the arcaded nave date from this time. Mind you, the pillars were nicked from the ruins of the Roman barracks at Caerleon. Waste not, want not.

The church was heavily restored in the Victorian era and was a Parish church until 1921, when the Welsh Church gained independence from the Church of England, though it still remains part of the Anglican Communion. St Woolos then became a pro-cathedral, which I take to be a sort of novitiate, and in 1949 was granted full cathedral status. In Newport, everything comes to him who waits. Eventually.

The tourist brochure insists that the visitor take particular notice of a statue on the west exterior of the cathedral, which is supposed to represent Jasper Tudor. He is said to have built part of the tower, though he is more famous for being the uncle and guardian of the future king Henry VII. He is also supposed to have built part of the castle and Newport seems particularly desperate to claim him. However, this particular statue won't do much to establish the truth one way or the other since it hasn't got a head. *Tant pis.*

Up Stow Hill, puffing a bit now. The great untidy hulk of the cathedral is at my right shoulder and the going is getting tougher. I try a gate and it's locked. Further along, the road flattens out a bit and there's another gate. Locked. Two men on the inside, among the graves, see me rattling the bars and one of them asks "Are you trying get in?" I reply in the affirmative with as much equanimity as I can muster and I'm told to go to the lychgate round the corner.

On the corner is an elaborate drinking-fountain erected by the Women's Temperance League to provide a plentiful supply of Adam's Ale for those who might try to get away with thirst as an excuse for supping something stronger. To my disappointment it is no longer working. Health 'n' safety strikes again? I eye the

pub across the road, which eyes me back, looking smug.

Through the lychgate and up the path to the main door of the cathedral. I turn the knob and open the door, which responds with a sacrilegious *bing-bong* like a corner shop. A chap in brown shoes and a very clean anorak scurries up and greets me like an eager merchant. What have I come for? Can he help me?

Um – two ounces of blind Faith, if you would be so kind, and a modicum of Grace... perhaps you'd put it on my account?

"I'm just looking," I say, lamely. "Have you been before?" he asks, and when I say it's my first visit he starts on the guided tour. "Woolos's real name was Gwynllyw and he was..."

So what was he, then? A king? A warrior? A barbarian? A pirate?

He runs through one of the tamer versions of the story. "A Saint." OK. I am still not quite sure who canonised him, but let it pass, let it pass.

"You will have noticed the arch as you came in..." and he continues his genial paraphrase of the guidebook until he suddenly seems satisfied on some point of inner debate. "I'll leave you to explore on your own – do ask if there's anything you want to know." Then suddenly, as if he must explain – "I'm sorry. I'm a volunteer from the Friends of St Woolos. We have to greet people. To be sure that they are genuine visitors. We have so many vandals."

I suddenly liked him very much. "That's fine," I said. And it was.

So what can I tell a reader about this place? For the architecture, the ground plan, the official history you can look at the guidebook or listen to your Friend. But don't miss the plain, uncoloured windows in the Galilee Chapel, beyond which the trees dance. And do allow yourself time to seek out the source of the light that shines from behind the altar. A small high window where two linked ladders try unsuccessfully to interrupt its ingress through glass that is stained with a hundred variations of a single primary colour; the least regarded, the most underused in this context. Make yourself enough silence to hear John Piper singing in yellow.

St Woolos Cathedral, Newport

Haphazardly conceived and ill-defended,
Against the odds it stands among the dead.
Made and unmade and carelessly extended,
An artless shippon with a lean-to shed.
Each little death has seen it rise again;
A monument one cannot but applaud,
As much to the pigheadedness of men
As to the greater glory of the Lord.
A later spate of damage-limitation,
Replacing broken tiles and rotten wood,
Included a mad act of exultation
Among the shoring-up and making-good
And through a round hole in its dreary skin
A beam of glory alleluias in.

THE MYSTERY OF THE WROUGHT IRON GATE

You know how it is; sometimes you see something that makes you catch your breath and look again, turn your head to hold it in your line of vision for as long as possible and close your eyes later to call it to mind again. I felt that way about the lovely wrought iron railings by the roundabout where Fields Park Road joins Risca Road, in which was set a decorative gate which opened onto a path which disappeared among trees. The sort of gate that tempts the child in a fairytale to step through to adventure.

Before I moved permanently to Gwent I visited often. Philip would pick me up at the station and drive me out along Fields Park Road and one day as we semi-circled the roundabout I asked him what was to be found through the wrought iron gate. "It's the burial place of

Proust," he said. "Not a lot of people know that."

"Bollocks," I thought, stifling a grin. "Take me there and show me?" I asked, innocently. His eyes remained firmly on the road ahead. "One day," he said. But I never held him to his promise, not wanting to spoil his joke.

Much later, after Philip's death, I was travelling the same route in a taxi and looked out as I have always done, for the magic gate in the beautiful railings. "What is the name of this place?" I asked. "We always call it Jews Wood Roundabout," said the driver, "but don't ask me why". So I didn't.

Even later, I asked another driver. "Because there's a Jewish cemetery in there", he replied, indicating the railings. My heart did a backflip. Could Philip have been serious after all? But I still didn't go there, just in case. Instead, on a trip to Paris, having taken some of Philip's ashes with me, I made enquiries as to the actual whereabouts of the mortal remains of poor Marcel.

In Search of Lost Proust

You used to tell me that Proust was buried
In Jews Wood Cemetery, Newport, Gwent.
Although I knew it was one of your wind-ups
Like the mythical town of Dickhead, Minnesota
I always secretly hoped it was true.

But I have found him now, in *Père Lachaise*
Irretrievably immured in black marble.
I have dibbled a hole in the gravel
Next to his tomb with a Swiss army knife
And carefully peppered a drift of ashes
Onto the slightly sour earth underneath.
Combing the small stones gently over you
With grubby fingers, I am celebrating
A fitting end to our *folie à deux*
And a fine way to win an argument.

But I still had to find the last part of the puzzle. Was my beloved making the whole thing up or was there, as I had begun to suspect, some basis for his assertion? I decided to make more enquiries as part of my ongoing researches for this book. Not taxi drivers this time, but the City Council, the road map and the internet.

I started with Google, as one does, and typed in 'Jewish Cemetery Newport' I was taken straight to a poem called 'The Jewish Cemetery at Newport'. I couldn't believe my luck! Much turgid reading later, I found that the poem was by Longfellow and that the cemetery in question was in Newport, Rhode Island. (It took courage to confess that.)

I found the roundabout on the map and discovered that the beautiful railings are those of Coed-Melyn Park. There was no cemetery marked there, though, only the mighty boneyard of St Woolos, adjacent to it. This was, when it opened in 1850, the first public cemetery in the UK. Researches told me that an application had recently been made to extend the big cemetery into the park to relieve overcrowding and that there had been vociferous local opposition to this. The park was saved, so surely there couldn't have been a cemetery there already? There was no mention of it. Nobody seemed to have heard of such a thing.

One last throw of the dice; I rang the man in charge of Newport's cemeteries and asked him if there were Jewish graves in Coed-Melyn Park. "Yes," he said. "There's an old cemetery by the gate, but it's been closed for a long time now. There's a newer plot further into the park." "Thanks!" I said.

So, up Stow Hill as far as the Handpost, a busy-looking pub which stands at the junction with two other roads, Risca Road and Bassaleg (say it *Baze*-leg) Road. Both of those roads lead to the district of Glasllwch (say it *Glass*-lock with a short 'a'). For me, of course, there was no real choice. Risca Road it had to be, knowing that it would lead eventually to the roundabout by the magic railings.

And it wasn't far. I had never approached the roundabout this way before, and never on foot. I was soon aware of St Woolos Cemetery over the wall on my left. The collection of mortal remains awaiting the last trump was indeed impressive. A hundred and fifty years of local mortality lay here, each corpse individually wrapped and planted, like a huge box of hand-made chocolates. If indeed, as some factions claim, there is a predetermined pecking order when it comes to admission through the pearly gates, the trump, when it comes, will be accompanied by the appearance of a mighty hand like the one Michelangelo painted. But this one will not be pointing majestically to the pleading outreach of Adam, it will be hovering beakily with finger and thumb over the top layer of foetid confectionery, looking for the aubergine creams.

But these dead were not the Chosen People whom I had come to find, so I ignored the little blue and white gatehouse that stood by a side entrance and headed for the roundabout, which I could now see clearly just ahead, and the magic gate in the remembered railings. *Oh, please, please let it be there; let it be open...*

The gate did not disappoint. The posts were tall, intricate boxes inside which rowan trees were growing, perhaps by accident. The finials were painted gold. Not recently enough to look opulent but tidy all the same. None of the horrible admonitions to keep dogs on leads and keep off the grass, just a discreet word to the wise: *beware uneven ground*. Somebody cares enough about the intrinsic beauty of the place to keep it safe; no asphalt paths, no flowerbeds. Only the great earthen floor with its overhead lighting filtered through the ancient beech trees, which were waiting for the secret signal to burst into their special shade of green.

But I didn't go straight to the beeches. Instead, I followed a simple, trodden path that went left, bordered by random primroses and wood anemones and skirted a lovely old wall, colonised by ferns and mosses, which I took to be the original boundary of St Woolos. I walked on. The noise of traffic had been overtaken by birdsong as they went joyfully about their seasonal business. Dull clumps of green spears promised fistfuls of bluebells at any moment. I was enchanted by this lovely place, just as the gate had always promised.

At the far end of the park I found a small crowded burial ground and through the wire fence I could see a simple redbrick building and make out Hebrew inscriptions on the stones. This was what I had come to find, but there was no obvious way in. It sat like a serious little solitaire in the overstated setting of the main cemetery, where the latest gentile graves, piled high with floral afterthoughts, cocked indecorous snooks at sobriety and meditation.

When I finally found the gate, it was padlocked. It was not difficult to see why. Vandals had given the place a good going over; sprayed graffiti and overturned headstones. Everything inside had

been sullied and spoiled. I walked round, looking up at the wall, the gates, and the windows of the burial house where the stained glass Stars of David could just be made out through protective mesh that sheltered them. Like so many urban, sacred places, it needed protecting from the disaffected, and they, true to form, had found a way of retaliating. Unable to break the windows they had desecrated the door. But it was the perimeter wall that broke my heart. As I walked round it I noticed the tall gate, daubed with black paint, the high red wall with no handholds and the five strands of barbed wire leaning outwards that reminded me suddenly, horribly, of Auschwitz.

Further round into the main cemetery again. The sun shone and windchimes twangled from a tree over a busy bed where lots of labels sprouted from the ground where ashes had been interred. A green hedge hid the harsh edge of the Jewish plot and there stood, with their backs to it, a row of headstones with inscriptions in Arabic. An attendant had come over to ask me if I was seeking a particular grave and I mentioned this, asking if they were Islamic burials. He nodded. I said it was strange to have put them alongside the Jewish ones and he smiled, "We call it our Gaza Strip". There was no disrespect in the remark and I smiled back. He was the person I had spoken to on the phone. I told him I was saddened by the state of the special cemetery I had come to find, and asked where the newer Jewish graves were. He explained that this was the new plot he had told me of, though it had been there sixty years. The old one was by the gate. Not the magic gate with gold finials by which I had entered the park, but the other gate I had passed on the way; the one with what I had taken to be a little gatehouse. The cemetery was behind the lovely old wall I had seen. He pointed the way but warned me sadly that this, too, had been broken into and vandalised. "It's kept locked," he said, "but there's a broken place in the wall hidden among the trees in the corner. It's where the scum broke in. If they haven't mended it yet, you might be able to scramble over." "Thank you," I said, "for trusting me."

And there, at last, I found it. The Jewish Cemetery, albeit without

Proust, small and solemn and pre-dating St Woolos by twenty years. It was just as I had imagined it; an exquisite walled garden with birds and sunlight and tall reverent trees. And crude black graffiti squirted over the white walls of what I now know to be a little synagogue. But I was peering at it through a locked blue gate daubed at head height with haphazard black, and as I stepped back from it after a long quiet look I felt a wrench and muttered "*ouch*". I saw that a clump of my hair was sticking to the gate. Anti-vandal paint. If you can't beat 'em, join 'em. I had had a lucky escape.

I followed the wall as my guide had suggested and came to the place where it had been pulled down. The old stonework full of vegetation and wildlife had been easy to destroy but on the inside new galvanised railings had been erected, their spikes dripping with the same angry black paint. I climbed up to them gingerly, but even so my right palm acquired a black diagonal stripe that stayed with me for several days. Carefully, through the railings, I photographed the sunny garden, the quiet old graves and the beer cans and the hideous daubings on the synagogue wall.

There was absolutely nothing in the drawings to suggest anti-Semitism or racism. Just the mindless smash it, sign it, claim it culture of unhappy youth, who believe that making your mark like a pissing dog has something to do with forever.

I did not go back through the magic gate in the special railings. I left the park by the small gate instead and went straight across the road to the bus stop, too sad to walk back into town. I sat on the low wall outside Stow Park Lawn Tennis Club, listening to the repetitive *whump-thwop* of a series of long rallies and looking at the black mark on the palm of my hand.

EAST

STEEL AND THE CITY

Steel is an alloy of iron and carbon. Steel typically contains between 0.3% and 1.5% carbon, depending on the desired characteristics. The addition of other elements can give steel other useful properties. Small amounts of chromium improves durability and prevents rust (stainless steel); nickel increases durability and resistance to heat and acids; manganese increases strength and resistance to wear; molybdenum increases strength and resistance to heat; tungsten retains hardness at high temperatures; and vanadium increases strength and springiness. Which is probably a good deal more than you wanted to know.

The *raison d'être* of the city's beloved Transporter Bridge was the ferrying of passengers over the river to and from the new Orb Steelworks on the East Bank which was being built by the Lysaght Company from the West Midlands. It opened in 1898. Between then and the Great War it flourished and grew huge, employing three-thousand men, all living in the Newport area. The Trannie ferried the workers from Pill, while over on the other bank new housing was created for employees, some of whom came with the company from the West Midlands. That's how the sidestreets off Corporation Road came to have names like Bilston, Dudley, Walsall and Handsworth.

In World War One the company produced trench plates, steel for helmets and brass for cartridges and, in World War Two, corrugated sheet for air raid shelters, sheet steel for helmets, ammunition boxes, jerricans, land mines etc, as well as pioneering the rolling of "duralumin" for aircraft production.

And between the wars the motor industry blossomed and the demand for sheet steel became so great that, in 1933, the UK's first mechanical rolling mill was installed.

Orb Steelworks has always been responsive to demand. In the early days the company had made a fortune with galvanised bathtubs. Now they specialise in electrical steels and since I didn't know what that meant I contacted them to

ask, which resulted in one of those conversations that are brought alive by somebody who knows and loves their work. The sort of person who couldn't be boring if he tried.

Electrical steels, it seems, play a vital role in the generation, transmission, distribution and use of electrical power and are one of the most important magnetic materials produced today. They are iron-silicon alloys and my informer explained that in most applications, silicon is an impurity and must be got rid of at all costs. But here it is vital in increasing the resistivity of the steel. Resistivity is the opposite of conductivity (but you knew that, didn't you!).

You can have grain-oriented steels, which I understand are manufactured with a grain, like wood, to minimise power loss. They are used in high-efficiency transformers. Or you can have non oriented steels, whose magnetic properties can operate every whichway. They are used for motors, generators, alternators and transformers which are not so important as to need the grainy stuff.

I was suddenly back in the physics lab in school, making an electromagnet. Winding copper wire round an iron core, then attaching the free ends to the terminals of a battery so that a flick of my switch made iron filings dance. Then trying it with different types of core. Aluminium was a non-starter, as I recall.

I remember finding out the hard way that the amount of current is critical and that a certain amount of the energy is lost as heat. The more current that flowed through the wire, the more heat was generated. Doubling the current increased the heat four times. Tripling it increased the heat nine times. So if the inclusion of silicon in the iron core can decrease the heat and increase the energy then... I pushed up my imaginary goggles and turned off my notional bunsen burner. Gottit.

Now I saw what the Orb man meant when he said that they had a "quiet smirk" when the discussion of green issues gave rise to pleas for energy saving, because "We've been doing it for years!"

A couple of days later I rang the mobile number he had given me to ask about the sources for the steel which Orb laminates and adulterates to such great effect. He told me it came from Port Talbot when possible, but much of the time the best price is sought on the world market. I apologised for the noise of clattering, because I was ringing from a callbox and mobiles cost money, which I was busily feeding into the slot with my left had as I made notes with my right. He said he was not aware of noise on the line because he was at home, outside, and somebody was shoeing a horse only yards from his door. The idea of such a long established application of the technology we were discussing made me smile to myself and I began to wonder what you'd add to a steel shoe to make the gee-gees run faster. But I'm willing to bet somebody has thought of that already.

Newport's biggest steelworks, state-of-the-art technology, employer of thousands, saviour of the town's economy, was built from scratch on a greenfield site on the east side of the river and went into production in 1963. It was meant to be called Spencer Works but is always referred to as 'Llanwern'. Originally it employed nearly ten thousand. Workers were brought in from parts of Europe and from elsewhere in the UK and the mighty blast furnaces produced steel non-stop, which was rolled and 'pickled' and rolled again. The works was designed with a capacity of two million tonnes of liquid steel.

When I first started visiting Newport at the end of the eighties Llanwern was the first landmark I looked out for as the train approached the town. That was where I got my coat down off the rack and started locating my gear for disembarkation. Dirty and ugly but hugely impressive, it was reminiscent of the industrial landscape of Teesside. I loved coming past after dark on winter evenings, when the glow of the processes made false sunsets and the flarestacks spat flame into the dusty sky. But they don't make steel at Llanwern any more. They stopped – just like that – in 2001.

They do other things, though. Steely things of a specialised nature about which I felt I should learn more. Quite early on in the preparation of this book I asked if I might visit the Llanwern works and was told that I should speak to Tom, who appeared at first to exist only on voicemail. Once or twice I spoke to him in person and he said he'd fix something up and get back to me. But he didn't. I left more messages. I began to feel that there was some deep secret reason why I shouldn't visit Llanwern and started fantasising about it. Remembering a scandal involving spiral welded pipes at Middlesbrough docks in the early nineties, I pretended that Llanwern was involved in making guns for Iraq and that if I found out for sure they would have to kill me.

So when one last request ended in an invitation to go and see for myself, I playacted for all I was worth. I was Lois Lane, invited to look into the lair of Lex Luthor. I would watch and listen. I would observe and extrapolate. I would speculate and verify. And if push came to shove I would shout for Superman.

However, I needed Superman far earlier in the proceedings than I had imagined. I needed to get to Llanwern by public transport. I rang Traveline Cymru to ask how this could best be done. They said they had no record of a steelworks at Llanwern. However, if I went to Newport and got on a number 61, a privately-run, two-hourly bus to Magor, I could ask to be put off at a stop called 'Llanwern Villa' which was the nearest they

could offer. It seemed odd, to say the least. I rang twice more and got the same answer. The last person I spoke to looked it up on a map and found the steelworks, but said that the stop appeared to be a long way from any obvious entrance and was separated from the works perimeter by a wide ditch. Marvellous. I would have to fly.

This sounded more suspicious by the minute. No easy way to get there by public transport. Protected by some sort of moat. I was starting to feel really scared. After all, even after the lay-offs the place still employs nearly five thousand souls. Surely some of them go to work by bus? Or are they held captive on-site? I began to ask myself if I really wanted to go there. But Tom sounded all right, and after all, Lois Lane would not let such a thing as mortal terror stand between her and the chance of a Pulitzer.

I got a bus to Newport and went into the transport company office, asking whether they knew of a better way to get to the works at Llanwern. "Yes," said a man in the queue – "run out and get on that bus there and tell the driver 'Tesco's'." Thus it was that I found myself, mere minutes later, outside Spytty Retail Park in Liswerry. I hitched up my rucksack and followed the signs to the steelworks. There is no substitute for local knowledge.

Traveline Cymru had struck again. But it's not altogether their fault. Once upon a time we had our own Southwalian office where they understood our simple needs, but someone rationalised the operation and now there's only one. And it's in Porthmadog. This means they have no idea what we monoglot Severnsiders are on about. They only know what's on their computer. The mysterious

Llanwern Villa, I later ascertained, is actually Llanwern *Village* but there wasn't room for the whole destination on their display.

My serviceable daps slapped the asphalt in time to the swinging of my arms. Eventually I arrived at the approach road to the gates of the works. There was a little hut with a bloke in it. A lighted display said it was operating at Security Level One, but whether this was good or bad I had no way of knowing. I trotted up like an eager puppy. "Can I ask what you want?" said the bloke. "I'm here to see Tom Johnson," I replied. He checked a list and smiled. "You're Ann Drysdale?" I nodded and was admitted. They didn't have to lift the stripey pole for me, I merely squoze past the end of it and headed for the building marked 'Reception'.

Here I found my luck had run out. I was given a long, hard look and found wanting. They didn't know a Tom Johnson. "Where does he work?" asked the reception man, and of course I didn't know. "Well, I can't ring him to tell him you're here unless I know where he is". "Ah" said I, "but I know his direct dial number so I can ring him on that payphone (I pointed). Then he can ring you and tell you where he is." "Do that, then," said he, and I hunted in my rucksack for the number that would assist me in *la recherche de Tom perdu*.

He came to collect me. I had imagined a stereotype steelworker and was amazed by a freshfaced graduate. He drove me in his car to the office block he inhabited and showed me into a small meeting room he had booked for my visit. On the table he had spread out a map of the works as it now is, with faint indications of what it once was. There were corporate magazines and handouts, a video and a TV to play it on. And within minutes of my arrival there appeared two cups of tea. The tea was good – but the cups were amazing!

They were neither boardroom bone china nor shopfloor heavy-weight half-pint jobs. They were rather small and tapered towards the bottom, like flower pots. The design was a simple one: two tickboxes – 'Without Milk' and 'Without Sugar' – and beneath these the further message 'Not Without You' and the explanation, Corus Teamwork. For now the works are part of Corus, a company formed in 1999 by an amalgamation of British Steel and the Dutch company Koninklijke Hoogovens. Tom saw me looking at the cups. He told me they were part of an ongoing culture change, which was known in the works as The Journey. I wasn't Lois Lane after all, I was Dorothy – and we sure as hell weren't in Kansas any more.

Tom introduced me to "one of the Old Guard" who had been at Llanwern for many years. Again I expected a heat-tanned, muscular, laconic macho, likely as not with bits missing – an eye, the odd finger, a whole arm even – but he was a good-looking, quiets-poken man in a very clean shirt who was doing a Master's in Business Management at Allt Yr Yn. He, too, was on The Journey.

When I had despaired of being allowed my visit, the wonderful Charles Ferris had introduced me to "someone who knew all about Llanwern", from whom I had heard all the stories of red hot metal and derring-do. My favourite was that any apprentice going to Porthcawl or Barry Island for a day out was required to bring back a stick of rock. His superiors would insist that he divide the length of the stick by the number on his shift and set up the rock in the rod-slicing equipment so as to cut it perfectly accurately into the required number of pieces with the minimum of waste. This was a story I had intended to share, but when Tom and his colleague continued their exposition on the importance of health and safety and 'housekeeping' (we don't leave dirty cups for someone else to pick up) I decided not to mention the rock and found myself mentally wiping the sticky bits off the machinery with a licked finger.

The two men explained that the old hierarchical system was gone, that each employee has responsibility for the whole company, that the managing director is approachable and the floor-worker can take concerns and suggestions higher through a series of ever-open doors. As the longtime partner of a management consultant I'd heard all this before and it wasn't as new as Tom perhaps supposed, but I bet it took time and a lot of angst to get it that far in a steelworks. I was impressed.

Tom took me on a tour of the site. In his car. We drove through the devastated 'heavy end' where the blast furnaces had been and where schemes for the re-use of the sixty-odd acres are still being chewed over by the city planners. There was a proposal for an airport at one stage, though now a small suburb seems to be favourite. We drove past the piles of steel slab that had been made in the other Corus plant at Port Talbot and brought by rail to await rolling. I was being taken to see them being rolled.

I was given a hard hat, glasses, a padded ear-brassiere and a lecture on safety procedure by the man who was to take us into the rolling mill. As we stepped out of the office I saw myself in a full-length mirror above which was written "The person responsible for my safety is…"

We watched from a high walkway. The hot slab came out of the reheating furnace onto a conveyor. It went through a series of processes to break up the 'scale' of oxides that had formed during the heating, was rolled and wriggled to make it clean, squeezed to make it flat and thin, had the end trimmed off to make it square and was sprayed with water to make it smooth. Because of all the protective gear I couldn't hear the roar of the machinery or see the shimmer of the heat. The only sensory organ unprotected was my nostrils and I was surprised to discover that a steel rolling mill doesn't smell of anything. I watched the last part of the process from the control room where a couple of men adjusted things according to computers, then went out to see the sheet rolled up and plopped off, still hot but shiny, into a yard for despatch. A man with gauntlets and a face mask came out, looked at the roll and marked it with a number. "Steve identifies each roll," I was told. I noticed a pile of offcuts and asked what they were. I was told that if the presenting end of the roll is unacceptably ragged, Steve will cut it straight. I asked what sort of equipment he used to calibrate the operation and I was told that he just cuts it with an acetylene torch. By eye.

I admitted to myself then that I had been a little disappointed by the rolling mill, but knowing about Steve and his experienced eye made up for it. I bet he can do a helluva good job with a stick of rock.

THE BEAR WHO PEELED ORANGES

Sometimes I hate myself. Again and again in the process of writing this book I have come across people who tell me wonderful things that I want wholeheartedly to believe, but am betrayed by my rattle-bag of a brain which squeezes out some piece of stored information that cries "bollocks!"

Whitson Court is a beautiful Georgian house between Goldcliff and Redwick, which was built, so I have been confidently told by more than one informant, by Beau Nash. When I was told in the bus station café, I choked on a chip and covered my confusion with a raised eyebrow and an implied "come again?" I was asked scornfully if I had never heard of Beau Nash, the Regency Dandy, "who built most of Bath". I repositioned my chip, chewed it contemplatively and washed it down with a mouthful of the best tea in Newport before I said, guardedly, "indeed", with a careful little upward inflexion calcu-lated to imply interest rather than disbelief.

It would have been churlish to point out that Beau Nash could not possibly have built Whitson Court. He was indeed a bit of a dandy and is almost synonymous with Bath. He was for a while the friend of the then Prince of Wales, but he died in the same year the future Prince Regent was born. His real name was Richard and he was a Welshman, born in Swansea. He studied at Oxford, served as a Guards Officer and studied law in London before pitching up in Bath in 1703 as *aide de camp* to Captain Webster, the Master of Ceremonies.

Bath's Master of Ceremonies was in charge of all the nightlife of city, overseeing balls and other entertainments (mainly gambling) and enforcing rules of etiquette so that it all ran smoothly and profitably. Captain Webster was killed in a duel, though I have been unable to ascertain with whom, and young Richard Nash took his place. He set about changing the social behaviour of the citizens, creating a strict code of conduct that made Bath a much safer and more pleasant place. He was called the 'Arbiter of Elegance', was given the nickname 'Beau' and became one of the most influential men in the social history of England. He found ways of circumventing the gaming laws until all gambling was made illegal in 1745, when his glittering career came to an end. He died a pauper, but even so was buried in Bath Abbey, for services rendered. But he was no architect and he never built so much as a brick shithouse.

John Nash, on the other hand, was a very famous architect indeed. He was the builder of dreams for his patron – the Prince Regent. He transformed the Brighton Pavilion into a south coast Taj Mahal and designed exquisite circuses, terraces and crescents. But not in Bath.

So there are two Nashes, conflated by local legend like the Gwynllyws of Wentloog. I have no reason to believe they were related. Beau couldn't have built Whitson Court, even as a one-off, since it was completed around 1795 and he'd been dead thirty years by then. But John – what about John?

Let's ask another John. John Newman wrote in *The Buildings of Gwent* that, although it has often been claimed that house is the work of architect John Nash "this is hard to believe". Hard, yes, if you think of John Nash, only as the darling of the Prince Regent who later transformed Buckingham House into Buckingham Palace. But not impossible.

For where was John Nash in the 1790s? Wales, that's where. And what was he doing? Well, he had come into some money in 1774 and chucked up his apprenticeship with the architect Robert Taylor. He retired (aged twenty-two!) to Carmarthen, but by 1783 he had lost it all and was declared bankrupt. So he started work as an architect again, specialising in country houses for the well-to-do gentry.

I think William Phillips of Langstone, prominent landowner and Member of Parliament, would have deserved such a definition. I like to think he'd have picked up on young Nash's growing reputation and engaged him to design Whitson House, as it was called then, just before his return to London and his meteoric rise to fame. I want to believe it, I really do. Partly for the honour of Newport, but mostly for the sake of my friend Charles Ferris, who owns the bus station chippie and who told me about the wrong Nash.

William Phillips built another house nearby, for his son who was soon to return from the American colonies. Alas, the young man never came back; his ship was wrecked in a storm and he drowned on his way home. The Phillips family foundered too, and in 1901 the house passed to a distant relative, the Reverend Oliver Rodie Vassall, who later took the name Vassall-Phillips. Joseph Bradney, in his *History of Monmouthshire*, writes that "this gentleman, being a priest of the Church of Rome, established a colony of French nuns in the house". He also wrote books, such as *Catholic Christianity; the Reasonableness of our Religion* and *The Mustard Tree; an Argument on Behalf of the Divinity of Christ*, for which Hilaire Belloc wrote an epilogue. So those who sniggered at the bit about the French nuns – *honi soit qui mal y pense*.

During the Second World War, there was a shortage of workers on the estate and for a while the house was home to two groups of helpers, one of Jewish refugees from Europe and another of German officer prisoners. Both would have been uneasy to know that the house itself was used as a landmark by German bomber pilots targetting Newport Docks.

Other refugees came. By the sixties the house belonged to a Mrs Mayberry who first of all gave houseroom to two bears, pensioned off from some local advertising duties and later to a lion called Claude. Then there were monkeys, and other big cats and the place operated for a while as Whitson Zoo. In the seventies, though, it was forced to close as a commercial enterprise and most of the animals were rehomed. I was told that some of them went to a zoo in Carmarthen but when I rang to find out if it were true I was told by the tourist information office that there was no zoo in Carmarthen and never had been. The woman I spoke to told me that I probably meant Caernarfon. "A lot of people make that mistake," she said, with a sort of combination of a hiss and a sneer that made me feel sneered-at and hissed.

I tried other zoos but nobody had ever heard of Whitson, so I thought carefully and decided that it is better this way. As long as there are people who remember the animals and tell their stories, then it really doesn't matter about tying up the loose ends. This way Claude stays forever in the long summer evenings when the flarestacks at Llanwern roared into life at the end of the day and he roared back, alone no longer, as the sounds of the jungle echoed again in his tatty old ears.

And Pepe the bear, who loved oranges and would cradle the tiniest tangerine in one huge paw, while with the other he peeled it exquisitely and ate it, a segment at a time, in clumsy slow motion. I like to think of him frozen in his moment, spitting the pips and feeling the drunkenness of things being various.

Whitson Zoo? It was there for a while and then it wasn't. End of story.

SOUTH

THE PIRATE AND THE PILL

Now if you want a perfect example of Newport's attitude to language, consider Pillgwenlly. Usually abbreviated to 'Pill', it is the correct name for the dockland area at the mouth of the Usk. It means the little inlet where Gwynllyw the pirate used to hide his boat. I was told this by a local person and when I asked in all innocence "Is this the same Gwynllyw who caused the cathedral?" I was told "Yes, indeed" and was then told all about 'his' son Cadoc.

But Woolo/Gwynllyw lived in the fifth century and the pirate, if he lived at all, did so in the twelfth. That gives him a putative lifespan of best part of a Methuselage. I don't think so. I think it was a different chap.

As with all these city myths, I have listened, deadpan, to as many versions as I have been offered and chosen the most appealing. That's what writers do.

My point being? Well, the name Pillgwenlly has been the subject of a similar arbitrary decision. Over years of cheerful consensus it has been pronounced Pill (like an aspirin) to denote the geographical feature that is common to both sides of the Severn, and Gwenlly with the soft double 'l' of the Welshman who owned it, however long ago. A lovely hybrid – the intertwining of two tongues in a consensual kiss.

I wrote that last sentence under the influence of drink, in a pub called The West of England, in Brunel Street, in Pill, in Newport, in Wales.

Written on the walls of the West of England

Rob bought Des a drink
2.12.04

                    Des bought Jen a birthday
                    drink only 2 days late.

Billy paid for a cab!!!

                    Victor bought a round
                    8.2.04

Stretch bought 2 rounds in a row 3.3.05

A TERRIBLE THOUGHT

Someone, looking through an early draft of this project, asked innocently "Could we be told the type of beer?" and I realised they couldn't, because I didn't know. I don't drink beer.

I had an awful flashback to a Plaid Cymru meeting where the wonderful Dafydd Wigley, whom God preserve, drew cheers from my community with the phrase "let's send a message to gin-sodden Surrey!" and a grue of cold fear trickled down my spine. You see, when I was in the West of England, thinking profound thoughts about the meeting of Nations, I was drinking gin and tonic. Does this make me a Bad Person?

THE TRANSPORTER BRIDGE

"Oh, Trannie, Trannie, you serve us well" – Terry Underwood

Until 1906, the only link between the east and west banks of the River Usk at Newport was the Town Bridge built of stone in 1800 and sited where wooden bridges had spanned the river since the twelfth century.

The reasons for the new bridge were commercial. The Revolution had arrived. The Town Corporation was keen to bring industry to Newport and there was talk of a sheet steel rolling works. As part of an agreement with the Lysaght Company, who were building the first of Newport's great steelworks – the Orb works – on the eastern side, they undertook to seek Parliamentary permission to provide "better communication for foot passengers and possible vehicular traffic between the two banks of the river".

A private firm was operating a small boat ferry, but the journey was not without risk and they actually lost a passenger or two. A special exhibition in the City Museum contained a contemporary press report of the mishap – and also furnished the poem by Terry Underwood quoted at the start of this chapter.

Newport Transporter Bridge was designed by the Frenchman, Ferdinand Arnodin. He called it a '*transbordeur*'. The design was chosen in haste when the success of Newport's docks looked threatened by the rise of the new docks at Barry. The bridge was officially opened in 1906 by Lord Tredegar. It measures 196 metres (645 feet) across, has a headroom of 54 metres (177 feet) and can carry up to six cars and one hundred and twenty people across the Usk.

The bridge was fully refurbished in the early 1990s and full details of the work done can be found on information boards by the little visitor centre, which purveys souvenir shopping bags and teddybears with pictures of the transporter and chocolate bars whose wrappers read 'bridge the gap'. Most of this information would be of interest only to engineers but I did learn that, as part of the process, "the saddles which support the cables at the tops of the tower legs have been grouted" – for which we should all be profoundly grateful.

One thing I do rather regret, though. As the final icing on the cake, the festoon lighting which had adorned the bridge since 1988 was replaced in 1995 by a floodlight system and one of my fondest memories of Newport was switched off at a stroke.

Those lights – a chain of bulbs slung around the frame – made the whole structure look like a half-hearted Christmas tree and the first reaction of most visitors was "aaah, bless!" because the whole string was never, ever, as far as I could recall, complete. Those bulbs were a target for the eagle-eyed and the disaffected, the sharpshooter and the chancer, not to mention a degree of natural wastage. It was a game, guessing how many bulbs would be out of commission at any given time and which they would be. It was a way of making decisions, like

reading one's stars or counting one's cherry-stones. I liked to think that Newport maidens would stand on the bank at dusk, mouthing silently – he loves me, he loves me not...

I learned later that all those bulbs had to replaced by hand and that an executive decision had been made to undertake the perilous climb and the meticulous fiddling only when the tally of busted bulbs reached a certain number. So to those of us whose who saw it every winter evening on the way home from work, the bridge would appear to rise and set over the river at extended intervals like an alien sun.

Jan Morris has written: "It is now one of the last two such bridges in the world, the other, an exact replica also by Arnodin, is still running at Rochfort" (sic). It is hard to argue with the doyenne of Welsh travel writers, but there's definitely one in Middlesbrough, spanning the Tees, which was built five years later and is still going strong.

* * * * *

Those who know and love Newport's Transporter Bridge call it The Trannie. I find this pleasing. The great butch structure, all steel and sinew, straddles the river with its hands on its hips, tricked out in cobweb mesh with its gondola dangling on wires that flip languidly from one whip hand to the other. Oh, hee-hee.

But its friends and supporters, its local cheerleaders, are mostly of a generation upon whom the modern overtones of the term are lost. And this is probably a good thing.

Ray who lives nearby and who loves the Trannie, goes back and forth on the gondola and is benignly proprietorial, like the strange people who ride the buses, never sitting down but always standing alongside the driver and conversing in transport-speak. I was introduced to him by the Secretary of the Friends of Newport Transporter Bridge, of whom I am now a member. And so it came about that I was allowed to shin up the south-westerly leg of the Trannie all by myself.

Here I go. Up, up, up the ungenerous steel steps which make the Eiffel Tower look easy, hooking my fingers into the holes in the waist-high mesh because it feels safer. Out onto the walkway and out across the Usk. Wonderful view of the mud. Peering down to see the gondola going by below and nearly losing the tips of my fingers as the hawsers slide by like cheesewire. From up here the conductor's little pavilion looks quite exotic – like Valentino's tent in *The Sheikh* – and I find myself speculating on the possibilities within. Lordy, am I cracking up?

Now I am walking on galvanised weld-mesh, like the longest cattle-grid in Wales. The holes, through which the outgoing Usk is horribly visible, are four inches by two and the metal that has knitted them into doilies looks peaky and thin. I tread on the joins; instinct tells me they're stronger than the middles.

Looking out into the estuary I can see one chimney – just one – blowing desultory smoke rings into the damp air. And one exquisite red brick building down among the sheds and rotting things. I promise myself I shall make an expedition to find it later. For now I concentrate on the precarious passage of the turbid river.

★ ★ ★ ★ ★

I have done it. I am now on terra firma on the east side of the Usk – but where exactly am I? I ask Ray and he starts to direct me towards the M4. It seems he, too, cannot easily conceive of a woman without wheels.

I board the gondola and swan back, east to west. Above me the steel web quivers, but now I skim the river at high-tide level accompanied by a white van. Invited by the conductor into the pretty pavilion I am shown the minimalist workings therein. Usually, he tells me, the gondola is driven from the motor house on the eastern end of the bridge itself. The seamless success of the enterprise depends on the presence of a bit of red rag tied round the mighty hawser that hauls the whole doings to and fro. When the red rag reaches the winding gear, the gondola is touching the west bank and the chap applies the brakes. Faultless technology; I am delighted.

"Have you been over the top?" asks the conductor. It has echoes of trench warfare. I nod proudly. "What a view, eh?" he says. "Did you see the jewel in the crown?" I look blank. "The stadium," he says. I look blank. "The Millennium Stadium," he says. "In Cardiff?" I ask, with a slow sadness dawning. He nods enthusiastically and I look up again at the towering Trannie so he can't see my face. Do people really climb three hundred wind-blasted ladder-rungs in Newport in the hope of getting a glimpse of Cardiff?

★ ★ ★ ★ ★

At that moment I was aware as never before of Newport's status in relation to the other two cities on the edge of south Wales. Cinderella on tiptoes, watching her sisters set off for the ball. I am writing this book, I realise, in the capacity of Fairy Godmother. I send a silent request to the centenarian Trannie – *help me!* Perhaps she will.

Who is to say that she will not one night loosen her stays and let it all hang out? She will stretch her glorious legs, straighten the seams of her mesh stockings and mince through Pill on spiky heels. (*Ooh – get her!*) Brunel Street – Alexandra Road – Commercial Road and then, pausing only to wink at the naked sailor on Gilligan's Island, she will carry straight on into the broken heart of the city. She will stop at

the Westgate Hotel, ugly after its botched face-lift, where a chalkboard now proclaims "Newport's only GLB night: Loud and Proud". Inside, she will take the stage to a roar of applause and by popular request she will do her favourite turn – *I Will Survive!* Go, girl, go!

TO THE LIGHTHOUSE

Today I do not go as far as the bus station; I get off the bus at the Ebbw Bridge and head for the West Usk Lighthouse. It is a classic case of taking the middle way, for the road winds prettily through the Gwent Levels, below the A48 which takes the serious traffic to Cardiff and above Docks Way, the broad dual carriageway which takes the heavy goods vehicles to the docks.

The concept of a being without wheels seems alien to the designers of traffic-flow systems on the city's fringes. I run like a rabbit between the juggernauts and dive for the safety of the Dyffryn roundabout, which turns out to have been recently reconstructed. Its consistency is that of soggy trifle sponge and my shoes are significantly countrified by the time I bolt across the last stream of traffic and take the by-road to St Brides.

Despite trees and a proper pavement, the road is obviously leading out of the city. Passing the Stonehouse, where I was wont to lunch wetly with my *Argus* colleagues, I tramp purposefully towards the sea. On my right the housing estate oozes mid-morning torpor.

At Duffryn High School civilisation as we understand it comes to an end. The pavement stops and is replaced by a muddy verge.

Running alongside the road and effortlessly keeping pace with it are the reens – the mysterious mini-canals of the levels, designed to drain and irrigate the flat lands that the Romans reclaimed from the sea and gave to the campaign veterans who chose not to go home. Land which has been farmed and cherished ever since.

It is winter and the reens are not at their best. A couple of quick recces to right and left is enough to show that the area is popular with the local people for a variety of reasons:

> What was he doing, the great god Pan,
> Down in the reeds by the river?
> The call of nature, the call of man,
> Had drawn him down to the bosky bank
> For a Jimmy Riddle, a J Arthur Rank
> A drag on a fag, or whatever…

The evidence of all of them is everywhere apparent, as is that of alfresco dining on local specialities of chips and cola.

On and on goes the road, over the railway and on towards Ely, with the character changing subtly as it winds past real working farms and cared-for cottages. And at last the turning to the lighthouse, left and seawards, a rutted shingly path more suited to a 4x4 than a middle-aged woman in sensible shoes.

The last stretch of the track is shared with cattle and my consequent hopscotch progress is observed with amusement by a man on a tractor. A final passage through a steel farmgate that swings and bounces, full of its own newness, and shuts behind me with a satisfying clang. And there it is. The West Usk Lighthouse, looking like a cotton-reel compared to the Eddystone, cheerfully ensconced on the estuary, where the broad mouth of the Usk sucks up to the Severn as together they seek to come to a twice-daily accommodation with the Celtic Sea.

It was built by the Scottish architect James Walker, at the junction of the estuaries of the two rivers at a time when large vessels came and went about their business in Newport Docks. And originally stood on its own island. The guide book says cheerfully, "But luckily for visitors, it is now possible to approach without getting your feet wet". I looked ruefully at my shoes.

The lighthouse was decommissioned in 1922 and the present owners, Frank and Danielle Sheaham, bought it when it was semi-derelict in 1987. They have lovingly restored it as befits its present purpose – arguably the wackiest and most wonderful bed and break-fast establishment in south Wales.

It was first brought to my attention when a colleague on the *Argus* wrote a piece about the first of the therapeutic installations – a flota-tion tank that was installed in the early nineties. It is still there; full of warm water saturated with mineral salts in which the client floats like a tourist at a Dead Sea resort or like the carcase of a pig, summarily released from agony and apprehension, bobbing in brine on the first stage of its transformation to bacon.

There was misunderstanding when I arrived. Frank, preoccupied, motioned me to a huge comfortable sofa and asked me to wait. A family were checking out, thanking him for his excellent hospitality. The little daughter, seeing me about to sink into the sofa, squealed delightedly "don't sit on him!" and pointed to a fairly lifelike stuffed cat curled up stiff on the cushions. This was clearly a running front-of-house joke. I picked it up by its tail and embarked upon the *Monty Python* parrot routine to the delight of the assembly. Out of the corner of my eye I could see a Dalek standing in recess beneath the stairs. It, in turn, appeared to have seen me.

Frank bustled by again and said Danielle wouldn't be long. On his third swift progress he apologised for his lack of hostliness and explained that he was waiting for an author who wanted to talk to him about the lighthouse and he was anxious that it should look its best.

I broke it to him gently and he was astounded, but rearranged his face with admirable swiftness. Something in my demeanour had convinced him that I had come to receive one of his wife's comple-mentary therapies, a speciality of the establishment, and he was waiting for something more in line with his expectations of authorli-ness. I forgave him; our tour began.

The lighthouse is on two floors with a diameter of fifty feet and walls nearly three feet thick. The slate-bedded entrance hall leads to a central spiral stone staircase over the original well that provided drinking water for the keepers. The first floor bedrooms are arranged like wedges of cheese around the perimeter, each room having a slightly different outlook over the low lying marshes and rivers. Steps lead up to the roof garden and the fifteen foot diameter lamp room, which was restored with grant aid in 1997 whereupon the lighthouse became a Grade II listed building.

Up here you can get the full 360 degree view. And what a view it is. Frank still seems unable to believe in the good fortune that has led him to live in this amazing place. The tides come rushing in twice a day, so the landscape is never the same. The sunrises and sunsets are spectacular. The full moon has to be seen to be believed – and the storms! Frank's eyes light up at the thought, but he is lost for words.

It is up here that Frank is currently working on a device associated with Electronic Voice Phenomena or Instrumental Trans-Communication. He is listening for ghosts or aliens or any attempts at transmission from other worlds. I thought about the Dalek and wondered, just for a moment, but as he explained the equipment and the importance of keeping an open mind I warmed to his enthusiasm. When I saw him he was hoping to hold a conference on this subject, on which he is now considered something of an expert.

Local farmers have made many UFO sightings near the light-house. There have been reports of inexplicable activity in the sky and one of the guests has taken a picture of a strange glow around the lighthouse. (Yes, the same thought occurred to me – but the great lamp itself is not working any more.)

Frank is eager to point out that the lighthouse isn't haunted but I found myself hoping that something exciting does get in touch. He is a nice man and he deserves it. I just hope that when it happens – as one day it surely will – the poor soul is not mistaken for a candidate for complementary therapy.

EBBW

> Or Ebbw's voice in such a wild delight
> As on he dashed with pebbles in his throat
> Gurgling towards the sea with all his might.

> From 'Days That Have Been' by W.H. Davies.

How interesting that Davies sees the Ebbw as masculine. Good for him; so do I. So much current writing, especially by women, identifies water as a female element, comforting, dangerous, changeable and profound. Maybe that applies to the Severn, personified by Milton as Sabrina, goddess-nymph of the river, or even the Usk, at a pinch. But not the Ebbw. He's a bloke.

Ebbw is the archetypal Valley Commando, sneaking and blustering by turns as he makes his way down to the city. On his way he picks up the Sirhowy at Crosskeys and I once went to the joining-place, to observe their coming-together, quite sure that I was going to be disappointed. One river joining another, eh? Bet it's not as simple as that. I'll bet there's *pipe*s. There are always pipes involved in these nominal unions. But when I found it I was delighted to discover that the Sirhowy just slipped over a weedy step into the Ebbw and the pair of them carried on, butties, arm-in-arm on their great adventure.

I have no way of knowing which bit of him Davies saw as his throat, but I have always thought of it as Ebbw Bridge on the Cardiff Road, where two arches span the water and the pillar between forms a chunky uvula that sometimes shimmers in the sunshine as though the river were singing.

Knowing that Ebbw doesn't actually make it to the sea on his own but rides piggy-back on the Usk into the Severn Estuary, I wanted to find out what happened when they met. So I followed him from Ebbw Bridge to see where he went. Not that it was easy. Docks Way sees to that. The main road has been fitted with a noise-abatement barrier to protect the riverside housing development below, so I lost sight of the river a few hundred yards from the bridge and took him on trust up to the point where the barrier stops and the Maesglas estate begins. The residents there are deemed immune to traffic-roar, I suppose. But when I peered down to where the river ought to have been, he'd gone. I could see him in the distance over the other side of the road. He had snuck underneath it a hundred yards back and I now had to get across the predatory dual carriageway. I decided that to make a run for it would be foolhardy, so I carried on parallel to his course and eventually came to a tunnel that took me under the road and out into a green open space with the Ebbw in view at the edge. A playing field.

But not a playing field in the sense of a marked-out, thou-shalt-play-footie sort of playing field; this was a field to play in and there's a world of difference. I followed a path down to the river, where it crossed a bridge and turned right into the Dyffryn estate. I turned left, into a sort of grubby heaven. All long the riverside great stands of wild balsam thickened the air with its syrupy scent and paths of beaten earth ducked and dived into clumps of gorse and clusters of bushes. Rough woodland held dens and secret hoarding places for found things, and through it all the Ebbw headed purposefully seawards despite being stoned enthusiatically by a gang of little boys who played around a pile of bikes like girls at a *Palais de Danse*, bopping round their handbags. When I got home that night, I

wondered where I'd been.

I discovered that the area appears to be listed on the realdaysout website as Llwyn Hirr (sic) and described as "roadside site at forest edge, sheltered by tall beech and larch woods". A map locates it exactly, alongside Docks Way. But there's no mention of the pebbly Ebbw, so I wondered if this was its real name, especially since the website gives 'Llwyn Celyn' exactly the same map and location, and I know that's Forestry Commission land not far from Caerphilly. Moreover, even after making a slight amendment to the Welsh spelling, the only Llwyn Hir I've ever heard of is the one in Mid Glamorgan where Ron Davies AM went to search for badgers in 1999.

I rang the Council, fighting my way past the Contact Centre. The Parks Department knew of the playing field, because they cut the grass, but as to the bit beyond, they didn't know what I was talking about and directed me to the Countryside Team. The Countryside man knew where I meant but had no name for it; it is just a left-alone, set-aside area for which there are no plans whatsoever. So even if it had a name, I probably wouldn't tell you, because I'd rather you didn't go there if it's all the same to you. It's mine. And Ebbw's.

And no, I didn't manage to follow the Ebbw as far as the Usk. I came to a blocked path with gates and admonitions. When I went in search of a possible permission-giver I drew a blank. But Charlie Ferris told me that he'd put me in touch with someone from Uskmouth Sailing Club who would be able to ferry me to it in style, though I haven't taken him up on it yet. After all, it could well turn out to be a disappointment. There might be pipes.

MAESGLAS AND THE NEWPORT SHIP

Murphy's Law, they call it. The certainty that anything that can go wrong, will.

Imagine you have just started to build a new Arts Centre

overlooking a tidal river. You have constructed a cofferdam so you can work on the waterside foundations and it's all systems go. A cofferdam? That's a structure created around a site of underwater building or repair operations, which can be drained to allow access – like a dry dock.

But with a dry dock, you rather expect to find a ship in it, whereas the ship they found at the bottom of the Riverfront cofferdam was a complete surprise, and not altogether a welcome one. They had sliced through the hull of a fifteenth century sailing ship. The prow and stern were outside the limits of the proposed excavations but the middle bit was there, with the mast step and the timbers showing clearly that it was, for its time, a very big ship indeed.

Now, suppose the new Arts Centre had been your project and you had just made such a discovery, would you throw your hat into the air and shout "Hurrah!"? I think not. Thoughts of schedules and completion dates and penalty clauses would pretty well guarantee a knee-jerk response of "Oh, *shit*" and a shifty glance over the shoulder to see who else had spotted it. Which was more or less what Newport Council did. They played down the find, authorised a brief examination, had the wreck dated (to 1465) and photographed. And then decreed that it should be reburied so as not to hold up the work on the Arts Centre.

There are precedents. When I was but a girl, developers in the City of London discovered an underground Roman temple to the soldiers' god Mithras. They, too, hoped to get away with a quick recce and then fill it in and carry on, but the huge surge of public interest kept extending the life of the dig week by week, until, despite the outcries and the protests of the Press, time finally ran out. The foundations were removed to be reassembled above ground and are now a sort of traffic island, like Newport's castle. The last of the artefacts, including the head of Mithras himself, snatched from the ruins before Mammon finally called 'time', were cleaned up and put on show in a London Museum. Now Bucklersbury House stands over the remains.

U.A. Fanthorpe wrote a moving poem – 'Queueing for the Sun in Walbrook' – describing the gradual appearance of the temple and the long line of Londoners that filed past, interested and amazed. She quotes inscriptions from the sacred place – *Mithras, the unconquered Sun; Sun invincible from East to West* – while noting wryly that the reconstructed foundations now stand in the wrong place and face the wrong way.

But she didn't quote the inscription on the altar itself: roughly, *Ulpius Silvanus, Veteran of the Second Augustan Legion, who joined the Brotherhood in Arausio, made this altar and so has kept his promise.* And if you've read carefully so far, you'll know that II Augusta was Newport's legion, based in Caerleon for over two hundred years. The tingle begins…

Arausio is now the town of Orange, in Provence, famous for its Roman remains. Many legionary veterans were sent there on retirement to live in the sun and grow grapes. The cult of Mithras was mostly followed by the Officer class. What if Silvanus' early service had been elsewhere? What if…? and I find myself struggling for a connection, for a stake in the past.

For that's what happens when discoveries are made. That's what made those Londoners camp out on the pavements and visit the slow, unlovely dig time and time again. That's what made the good citizens of Newport, with the backing of the Press, shout so loudly for the saving of their ship that the Council had to listen and the remains of the vessel, scheduled to be buried in hasty hugger-mugger, have been almost entirely lifted and preserved. Power to the people! That's how Newport got its Arts Centre and, in a few years time, will have its ship, too.

Not that it was achieved without a struggle.

The wreck was discovered in June 2002 and the Council's initial proposals were disclosed. A public demonstration, which included a twenty-four hour vigil and a flotilla of small boats from the Uskmouth Sailing Club, secured a three million pound donation from the Welsh Assembly and a promise at the end of August that the ship would be "saved". However, it soon became apparent that this

promise was not all it appeared. By September the Friends of the Newport Ship were formed and fighting. They issued a press release bringing the Council's vacillations to the notice of the City. Conflicting statements were exposed – "The bow and stern of the ship are not our immediate priority"; "The remaining timbers won't be harmed if we leave them where they are"; and, almost unbelievably, "it's not worth recovering the whole ship because it wouldn't fit in the display area under the Arts Centre..."

Many of these Goldfish were donated to the Newport Ship Project Centre by Mrs Christine Bailey and her Daughter Sara in memory of their late Husband and Father Trevor John Bailey who died on May 29th 2004 whose Pond was his Pride and Joy

But the bow would give shape to the ship, perhaps even a name, and the stern would reveal the steering mechanism. And of course the timbers would be harmed; they'd been severed by the steel sides of the cofferdam and their relationship to the water and the mud that had preserved them thus far had been irretrievably altered. And surely, in the ten to fifteen years that it would take to reassemble the ship, a place appropriate to its final size could be contrived? One or two of the Friends mischievously suggested that perhaps it would be a better use of the ghastly conversion of the Market Hall. I was inclined to agree.

On the 19th April 2003, the Daily Telegraph reported:

> The excavation of a 15th-century ship, described as the most significant discovery since the Mary Rose, has descended into recrimination and threats of legal action.
>
> With at least 95 per cent of the ship recovered, a dispute over whether to rescue the rest has led to accusations of "cultural vandalism" against the Labour-controlled council in Newport, South Wales, while conservationists have been accused of putting the survival of the town's Victorian dock at risk.
>
> The identity of the craft remains a mystery, despite the discovery of artefacts, including timber bowls, leather shoes, woollen clothing and coins. It is believed the craft, which was probably built in the 1460s, was a trading ship that had been docked on the Usk for repairs to a damaged mast. The shape of the timbers suggests that its appearance was a cross between a caravel and a Viking longship.
>
> Nobody from the council was available for comment but a spokesman for the Mary Rose Trust, which has advised Newport Council, said the decision was on safety grounds. "Our advice is that it could not be done without damaging the dock wall," a spokesman said. "What has been recovered so far is already very interesting."

Theories and speculations abounded. One of the jollier ones was that the ship had been moored at Newport for appearances' sake while some illicit cargo was ferried in little boats to Bristol under cover of darkness. Excitement grew.

Meanwhile, Bob Trett, chairman of the Glamorgan Gwent Archaeological Trust, was researching further afield. He found evidence that the ship was being repaired at the time but essentially was abandoned. And that it may well have been the property of Richard Neville, the Earl of Warwick, known as The Kingmaker because of his influence in royal circles and the part he played in deposing King Edward IV after the Battle of Edgecote in 1469. Warwick freed Henry VI the following year and restored him to the throne.

"Timbers found under the ship have been dated to no later than 1468 so therefore the ship must have been abandoned in that year or soon after," Bob Trett found. "When it was brought to Newport at that time, they started to repair the ship. We have a document from the Warwick records offices, which indicates that he was paying for work on a ship in Newport in the following year, 1469."

Mr Trett said that pirates operating under the Earl's sponsorship may have captured the ship from a previous owner, since it was a wild and unruly time and Warwick was using his own fleet for piracy to boost his finances. "Large numbers of Spanish, Portuguese and Breton ships were captured by Warwick's pirates. Evidence suggests our ship came from Portugal." He also surmises that the Earl of Warwick's death may have been the reason the ship never sailed out of Newport.

A warehouse on the Maesglas Industrial Estate was chosen to house the pieces of the wet, wooden jigsaw, and a team, under the leadership of marine archaeologist Kate Hunter, formed to examine it.

Early in 2004 the BBC's *Timewatch* team made a programme about the ship, featuring the objects found in it – a shoe, an archer's wriststraps, a handful of coins. And then came two more financial discoveries in quick succession. A grant from the Heritage Lottery Fund in December 2005 and the discovery, in February 2006, of a silver coin, found embedded in the keel of the ship, where the two main timbers were joined together. Copper coins were ofteninserted at these points to stop decay, but this was silver.

It was probably part of the keel-laying ceremony. This makes perfect sense to me. I don't know whether they do it in Wales, but in

England, where I grew up, it is traditional for adult visitors to wrap a piece of silver in the tiny fist of new baby 'for luck'. And this ship was once somebody's baby too. The coin is French and was wrapped, brand new, in tarred cloth and a little hole was made to hold it, like a blessing, safe in the heart of the new ship.

So the Newport Ship was probably built in France. Probably; possibly – these are the words of archaeological research and long may they resound in a world that howls for certainties. But the fact that things and theories change is part of the fun of it. Since the story began unfolding, artists having been giving their best guesses as to what the ship looked like and as each new piece of evidence makes nonsense of the last, the 'definitive picture' changes. These artists' impressions now run into double figures and there is a running joke among the Friends that, when they arrive at number forty, they will have a nuclear submarine.

Come to think of it, the statement from Newport Council after the discovery of the coin demonstrated a *volte face* from their initial stance that almost beggars belief:

> The whole restoration of the Newport Ship is an exciting journey in itself, and I am sure this latest find is one of great significance. We look forward to many more discoveries as the project continues its excellent progress.

And continue it does, in the warehouse at Maesglas, down behind the sorting office, where the teams of young archaeologists work alongside the latest recruits to the preservation game – the busy goldfish that swim among the timbers, nibbling the animal and vegetable encroachments to which the ancient wood is open, now that it is no longer protected by the city's kind, conserving mud.

THE NEWPORT WETLANDS

Not like the brand-new Bay of Cardiff fame,
With jewelled arms conjoining land to land;
Here at our sea-washed sunrise gate shall stand
A mighty mudflat with a boring name
And marsh-gas as her only guiding flame.
She was the nearest dumping-ground to hand
When Cardiff commerce issued the command
That took their tidal reaches from the frame.

"Keep, Cardiff folk, your vaunted Bay!" cries she
With silent lips. "Give me your migrant poor,
Your muddled masses yearning to breed free,
The feathered refuse of your teeming shore.
Send these, the homeless, tempest-tossed, to me,
My reeds and grasses frame an open door!"

No, that isn't what's written on the inaugural monument in the Wetlands Reserve. But if they've had the foresight to ask me, it would've been.

Instead, the shiny black stone of alien provenance that stands at a meeting of paths, states more prosaically that "this major reserve was acquired, designated and implemented in mitigation for the removal of the Taff Ely SSSI" and that it was a "joint project of the Land Authority for Wales, the Countryside Council for Wales and the Cardiff Bay Development Corporation, funded by the latter body".

There is no mention of Newport and there is a busty mermaid in the place where the flying monkey ought to be. I was surprised by a sudden wave of resentment on behalf of my city. After all, as has been stated forcefully elsewhere, *Newport isn't Cardiff*, and I shouted that out over the indistinguishable waters of the Usk and the Severn, which lay like misted sheet metal between me and St Brides.

When the reserve was established in 2000, there were rumblings from Newport's barrage lobby to the effect that Cardiff had somehow pulled a fast one but since then attitudes have subtly changed. The reserve is now owned and managed by a partnership of the CCW, the RSPB and Newport City Council. And the name of Newport is now included in the title almost by tacit agreement. It's all to do

with ownership and participation, but working at the level of mother wit, rather than clearly documented like the New Culture at Llanwern.

Geographically the reserve covers over four hundred and thirty eight hectares of the Gwent Levels from Uskmouth to Goldcliff, and the reedbeds, saline lagoons, wet grassland and scrub attract a variety of wetland birds. But then, they always did. The whole area of the levels has been made by man, who has battled with the sea for possession of it since Roman times. To some the flat, wet landscape can appear monotonous and when the tide is out the borders of wrinkled mud can seem downright ugly, but the whole area is an environmental and archaeological treasure. The difficult bit is persuading mankind to call a halt to his interference and leave it alone for a while so both birds and man can revel in the status quo. For not only have the dispossessed birds begun to gather here, they have been followed by small flocks of birders and twitchers who return on a regular basis to get their sightings of the visitors.

Here be ducks – not just your common-or-duckpond ducks, but shoveller, teal and pintail who are attracted to the wet grassland, and the large area of reedbeds, artfully aided and added-to, has attracted water rails and the almost-extinct bittern, whose East Anglian habitats are under threat. These do not breed here yet, but they will.

Comparisons with the successful reserves elsewhere in the UK have calmed fears that the land is somehow being 'wasted' and its potential as a real attraction for Newport is being taken seriously at last. There is real evidence for this. Just when it was beginning to win over the opposition an old enemy reared its head and the proposal for an M4 relief road which was believed to have been abandoned in the 90's surfaced once again.

On 15th August 2005, the RSPB issued the following press release:

> The Welsh Assembly Government has given its support, in principle, to a relief road which would run south of the city of Newport and across the Gwent Levels SSSI, a nationally important site which is Wales' largest coastal floodplain grassland site and amongst the best four sites of its type in the UK. We are likely to object to this project when consents are applied for, on the grounds of damage to a nationally important site for nature conservation...

And on 29th June, 2006 a press release from Newport City Council stated that:

> The route of the £350 million M4 relief road has been confirmed by the National Assembly. The new route is being proposed in response to environmental concerns; it will skirt the city rather than cut through a swathe of the Gwent Levels...

Nothing, of course, is safe till the fat lady sings and the bittern booms from the reedbeds of the Severn Estuary. But meanwhile the town that was built with its back to the river is now a city, slowly turning round to look at its reflection in the water and perhaps even to like itself at last.

I wandered a long time in the Newport Wetlands, blissfully alone except for the indigenous wildlife. Apart from one warning about getting too familiar with the giant hogweed, and another about the inadvisability of getting into deep water, the place is refreshingly free from notices and admonitions. Here and there are seats, some of them with thoughtfully placed rails to rest a notebook, or even a novel.

In among the reeds by one of the ponds a desperate squeaking desecrated the peace of the afternoon. A little coot had got separated from its family like a toddler in a shopping mall. One parent shot out into the middle of the pond and put on a display of acrobatics to distract my attention while the other headed for the reeds, muttering "Shut up, you silly little bugger; you'll alert the Dark Side..." I watched till the party were safely reunited. There was all the time in the world.

And here at the outward edge of the city you can find all you need to know about time and change. Neither seem frightening any more.

At the far end of the reserve lies Uskmouth Power Station, which donated some of the land. Here is generated enough power to supply the city and alongside coal they are proudly burning 'biomass' – wood-waste and olive pulp and pellets formed from the shells of the nuts that are crushed for the oil to make emollients for the skin. I wondered what the Romans did with their olive waste.

Romans? Mere parvenus! Out there in the estuary mud they have found mesolithic footprints. It pleased me to think that future mud-grovellers may one day stumble across that inaugural stone and wonder at its meaning. After all, the intentions of Sir Geoffrey Inkin O.B.E. were not so far removed from those of Ulpius Silvanus who built the altar to Mithras. The subtext of guilt and atonement will one day be just another matter for academic speculation, and this is exactly as it should be.

Perhaps the mud is as near as we get to forever.

Mud...

You knows it, clart! – Goldie Lookin Chain

You knows it, Newport citizen; you knows the special thud
Of the sound of builders' rubble being fly-tipped into mud.

Throughout the city's history its folk have known it, too
Though the Romans called it *lutum* and the Normans called it boue.
But I have lived in foreign parts, where farmers tend their sheep in it
And six long months of every year are always spent knee-deep in it.
Here there's a sort of sacred mud that holds a farmer's roots
And often holds the farmer too, by sucking at his boots;
A special, silky sort of mud that smells of cattle-farts
Which has been known for centuries oop in t'North as "clarts".

So blessings, Goldie Lookin Chain, from Newport's sons and
                                                    daughters
For naming us and claiming us for Usk's occluded waters
Whose coming in and going out is echoed in our blood:
We are the Estuary folk, the Children of the Mud!

THE PHOTOGRAPHS

Works Consulted

Black, C.V. *Pirates of the West Indies,* Cambridge University Pres, 1989
Davies, W.H. *A Poet's Pilgrimage,* Jonathan Cape, 1940
Davis, Haydn *The History of the Borough of Newport,* 1998
Grant, Allan and Chris *The Castle Companion,* Village Publishing, 1991
Morton, H.V. *In Search of Wales,* Methuen, 1936
Roberts, W.A. *Sir Henry Morgan: Buccaneer and Governor,* Kingston, Jamaica: The Pioneer Press. Hansard, 1952

Websites:
www.data-wales.co.uk
www.earlybritishkingdoms.com
www.paulflynnmp.co.uk
www.thenewport

And thousands of words of mouth over hundreds of assorted beverages.

Acknowledgements

Thanks are extended to Paul Flynn MP for his permission to use his personal website as a resource and to Harry Chambers of Peterloo Poets, who has given his blessing to my occasional quotation from my own previously published work..

To the Arts Officers at Caerphilly CBC for permission to quote from 'A Journey Around Caerphilly' produced by poet Francesca Kay and local schoolchildren for National Poetry Day 2001.

To Mike Buckingham and Charles Ferris for unstinting friendly assistance. To Gary Tolley and Peter Rose of Orb Steelworks and to Tom Johnson and his colleagues at Llanwern, for explanation without condescension.

Index